AMERICAN COOKBOOK

Favorite Classic Diner Recipes to Make at Home

(The Complete Guide and Recipes for Native American Cookbook)

Mark Phillips

Published by Sharon Lohan

© **Mark Phillips**

All Rights Reserved

American Cookbook: Favorite Classic Diner Recipes to Make at Home (The Complete Guide and Recipes for Native American Cookbook)

ISBN 978-1-7776245-0-7

All rights reserved. No part of this guide may be reproduced in any form without permission in writing from the publisher except in the case of brief quotations embodied in critical articles or reviews.

Legal & Disclaimer

The information contained in this book is not designed to replace or take the place of any form of medicine or professional medical advice. The information in this book has been provided for educational and entertainment purposes only.

The information contained in this book has been compiled from sources deemed reliable, and it is accurate to the best of the Author's knowledge; however, the Author cannot guarantee its accuracy and validity and cannot be held liable for any errors or omissions. Changes are periodically made to this book. You must consult your doctor or get professional medical advice before using any of the suggested remedies, techniques, or information in this book.

Table of contents

Part 1 1

Introduction 2

Recipes From The Northeastern States (New England) 4

   1 – New England Clam Chowder 4

   2 – Boston Baked Beans 7

   3 – East Coast Seafood Soup 9

   4 – Brooklyn Nyc Penne Arrabiata 11

   5 – Atlantic Coast Crab Cakes 13

   6 – Southern Baked Chicken 15

   7 – Cajun Jambalaya 17

   8 – Blackened Catfish 20

   9 – Loaded Grits 23

   10 – Southern Style Biscuits Gravy 25

   11 – Chicago Deep Dish Pizza 27

   12 – Kansas City Bbq Ribs 30

   13 – Chili, Cincinnati Slow Cooker Style 33

- 14 – Midwest Meat Loaf ... 35
- 15 – Pork Tenderloin ... 37

Recipes From The Historic American Southwest ... 39

- 16 – Black Bean Soup ... 39
- 17 – Southwestern Chicken Quesadillas ... 41
- 18 – Lasagna, Tex Mex Style ... 44
- 19 – Southwest Rice Vegetable Casserole ... 47
- 20 – Pork Chile Posole ... 49

Favorite Recipes Of The American Pacific Northwest ... 51

- 21 – Smoked Salmon Scramble ... 51
- 22 – Northwest Prawn Spinach Pasta ... 53
- 23 – Pacific Razor Clam Chowder ... 55
- 24 – Raspberry Arugula Salmon ... 57
- 25 – Baked Oysters ... 59
- 26 – Hopi Stew With Dumplings ... 61
- 27 – Seminole Fried Tomatoes ... 64
- 28 – Sisters Stew ... 66
- 29 – Cherokee Beef Pepperpot Soup ... 68

30 – Navajo Chili 70

Connecticut - White Clam Pizza 73

Delaware - Boiled Crabs In Garlic Butter 77

Florida - Honey And Orange Glazed Grouper 79

Georgia - Brown Sugar Pork Chops With Peach Bbq Sauce 81

Hawaii - Steamed Mahi-Mahi Laulau 85

Idaho - French Potato Casserole 88

Conclusion 91

Part 2 93

Chapter 1: Autumn Season Breakfast Recipes 94

1) Pumpkin Oatmeal 94

2) Cinnamon Scones 96

3) Sweet Potato Omelet 98

4) Oven-Baked Egg Wraps 100

5) Applesauce Oatmeal Pancakes 102

Chapter 2: Autumn Season Lunch Recipes 104

1) Squash & Cilantro Fall Soup 104

- 2) New England Style Chowder 106
- 3) Cream Of Hash Browns Fall Casserole 108
- 4) Pumpkin Soup 110
- 5) Pumpkin Autumn Chili 112

Chapter 3: Autumn Dinner Recipes 114

- 1) Autumn Baked Whole Chicken 114
- 2) Apple & Cheddar Autumn Stuffed Chicken Breast 116
- 3) Turkey Pot Pie 119
- 4) Country Time Chili 122
- 5) Autumn 3 Bean Vegetarian Chili 124
- 6) Shrimp Tempura 126
- 7) Autumn Meat Loaf & Oats 129
- 8) Fall Spinach Salad 131
- 9) Fall Pumpkin & Chicken 133
- 10) Autumn Pumpkin Curry 136
- 11) Autumn Lo-Mein 139
- 12) Fall Shiitake & Pasta 142
- 13) Autumn Beef With Mushroom Sauce 144

Chapter 4: Autumn Dessert Recipes 147

    1) Autumn Apple Crisp 147

    2) Favorite Autumn Apple Dessert 149

    3) Fall Pumpkin Pie 151

    4) Fall Rhubarb Dumplings 153

    5) Fall Time Muffins 155

Alabama - Pecan Crusted Sweet Potato With Sour Cream 157

Alaska - Caribou Stroganoff 160

Arizona - Navajo Taco 163

Arkansas - Possum Pie 167

California - Grilled Artichokes With Californian Avocado 170

Colorado - Classic Denver Omelet 173

Conclusion 175

Part 1

Introduction

How can you integrate American foods into your recipe repertoire at home? Can you seek out the different varieties of ingredients you'll need to make these dishes? Are you curious about the various ways in which American foods can make your recipes tastier?

The regions in this cookbook include the Northeast, South, Midwest, Southwest and the Pacific Northwest. I have also included a section for Native American recipes, which can truly be called "American", since they were here long before immigrants landed on the shores.

The Northeast offers wonderful seafood dishes, especially in New England. Lobster and clam chowder are quite popular.

In the South, fried foods are king. But they also have many heavy and rich soup and stew recipes, and wonderful comfort foods.

The farmers of the Midwest grow much of the wheat, corn and soy grains for the American people. Much grain is shipped overseas, as well. The local foods are largely simple and hearty.

In the Southwest, many dishes are influenced by Mexico. Some of the ingredients used here include avocados, rice, beef and beans.

The Pacific Northwest region of America has some of the best seafood on the west coast. They are as proud of their seafood dishes here as the New Englanders in the Northeast.

Flip through this American cookbook and find some new favorite meals for you, your family and friends.

Recipes From The Northeastern States (New England)

1 – New England Clam Chowder

This is a wonderful dish to share in the chilly months of winter, and winters in New England can get pretty bad. Clam chowder is a staple food in Boston, but people in other areas of America enjoy the chowder, too.

Makes 4 **Servings**
Cooking + Prep Time: 1 & 1/2 hours
Ingredients:

- 1 1/2 tsp. of salted butter, softened
- 1/2 lb. of bacon

- 2 sticks of celery
- 1 onion, large
- 1 bay leaf
- 3 cloves of garlic
- 3 cooked, diced potatoes
- 2 fresh sprigs of thyme
- 26 oz. of clams, minced, with juice
- 1/2 tsp. of pepper, WHITE
- 2 1/2 tbsp. of flour, all-purpose
- 1 tsp. of Worcestershire sauce
- 1 cup of cream, heavy
- 1 1/2 cups of half half
- 3/4 tsp. of salt

Instructions:

1. Cook bacon till crispy in large pot. Remove bacon. Set aside and leave the bacon fat in the pan.
2. Add butter to bacon fat in pot. In it, sauté the celery and onions for three to five minutes.

3. Add potatoes, thyme, pepper, bay leaf and garlic. Cook till they are soft.
4. Add the flour next. Do it slowly, so it won't form any lumps. Cook for about five minutes.

5. Strain the minced clams from juice. Reserve both. Stir in the reserved juice and add Worcestershire sauce. Bring pot to boil.

6. Reduce heat to med. Simmer for 12-15 minutes. Add cream and half half. Simmer for 8-10 minutes.
7. Add bacon and reserved clams. Serve warm.

2 – Boston Baked Beans

There are more than a few baked bean recipes in the Northeast, but Boston baked beans is probably the most well-known and often imitated. The ingredients are simple, like bacon, beans and molasses, but the flavor is awesome.

Makes 6 Servings
Cooking + Prep Time: 4 hours 45 minutes
Ingredients:

- 1/2 lb. of sliced bacon
- 2 cups of navy beans, dry, soaked in water overnight
- 2/3 cup of diced bell pepper, green
- 1 sliced onion, medium
- 1 x 8-oz. can of tomatoes, diced
- 2 minced garlic cloves
- 2 tbsp. of coconut sugar or Stevia

- 3 tbsp. of molasses
- 1/4 cup of orange juice
- 1/4 cup of maple syrup
- 1 tbsp. of Worcestershire sauce
- 1/4 tsp. of mustard powder
- 2 tsp. of salt, kosher

Instructions:

1. Preheat the oven to 325F.

2. Simmer beans in the water you soaked them in overnight, till barely tender. This takes about one to two hours. Drain. Reserve liquid.

3. Arrange beans in casserole dish. Place portion of them in bottom, and then layer beans with onion and bacon.

4. Combine orange juice, Stevia, Worcestershire sauce, tomatoes, mustard, kosher salt, ground pepper and molasses in sauce pan. Bring to boil. Pour on beans.

5. Pour in barely enough reserved bean-soaking water to cover beans. Cover dish.

6. Bake dish for three to four hours in 325F oven. Beans should become very tender but not fall apart. Uncover halfway through your cooking time. Add additional liquid, if needed, so the beans don't become too dry. Remove from oven. Serve hot.

3 – East Coast Seafood Soup

Here is a meal that is simple and light at the same time. It's made with shellfish and fish that are simmered in tomato broth. It is sometimes referred to as a bouillabaisse. It is quite delicious.

Makes 8 Servings
Cooking + Prep Time: 90 minutes
Ingredients:

- 1/4 head of chopped celery
- Olive oil
- 1 peeled, sliced onion, Spanish
- 1 tsp. of thyme, diced
- 2 cups of wine, white
- 1 tbsp. of garlic, minced
- 2 quarts of diced, peeled tomatoes
- 1 1/2 lbs. of steamed, cut lobster

- 1 splash of sherry
- 1 lb. each of sea scallops, peeled, de-veined shrimp, sea bass and cleaned, scrubbed mussels
- 1 chopped stalk of parsley for garnishing

Instructions:

1. Brown the celery and onion in a bit of olive oil in sauce pot with heavy bottom. Cook till their color is a golden brown.

2. Add thyme and garlic. Add tomatoes and white wine. Simmer for 1/2 hour.

3. In another pot, of a sufficient size to hold your lobster, add two inches of water and bring it to boil.

4. Submerge the lobster in pot, head first. Cover. Steam for eight to 10 minutes. Shell should become bright red.

5. Adjust the heat so you can steam without the water bubbling over. Cut lobster in shell with chef's knife. Add to the mixture.

6. Add the rest of the fish to mixture. Gently simmer for six to seven minutes. Add sherry.

7. Garnish. Serve promptly.

4 – Brooklyn Nyc Penne Arrabiata

Pasta al arrabiata sounds elegant, but it simply means that this dish is made in tomato sauce. It's an easy pasta dish to make, even on busy weeknights.

Makes 6 **Servings**
Cooking + Prep Time: 55 minutes
Ingredients:

- 6 sliced garlic cloves
- 1/2 cup of oil, olive
- 1 x 28-oz. can of tomatoes, diced, with oil and garlic
- 1 tsp. of pepper flakes, red
- 1 chopped bunch of basil, fresh
- 1/2 cup of tomato sauce
- 2 eggs, large
- 1 x 12-oz. pkg. of penne pasta, dried
- 1 tsp. of garlic powder
- 2 cups of breadcrumbs
- 1 lb. of chicken breast cutlets, thin

- 1 tsp. of salt, kosher
- 1 tsp. of black pepper, ground

Instructions:

1. Heat 1/4 cup oil in large sized skillet on med. heat. Add garlic. Sauté for several minutes.

2. Sprinkle on pepper flakes. Sauté for a minute more. Pour in tomato sauce and diced tomatoes. Add basil. Stir occasionally while simmering for 18-20 minutes.

3. Bring large pot of salted water to boil. Add pasta. Cook for six to eight minutes, till pasta is tender, and then drain.

4. Whisk the eggs with fork in small sized bowl. Place the breadcrumbs in separate bowl. Then stir salt, ground pepper and garlic powder into breadcrumbs.

5. Dip the chicken cutlets into egg, then into breadcrumb mixture to coat completely.

6. Heat the last 1/4 cup oil in large skillet on med. heat. Fry the chicken for five minutes on each side. Coating should be dark brown in color.

7. Remove the chicken and slice it. Toss slices into sauce. Simmer for 8-10 minutes. Add cooked pasta and stir. Simmer for several more minutes. Serve hot.

5 – Atlantic Coast Crab Cakes

The Atlantic Coast is known for tasty crab cakes. This is a simple recipe, and easy to follow, and it will offer you the same basic tastes that New Englanders love so well.

Makes 9 crab cakes
Cooking + Prep Time: 1 hour 10 minutes
Ingredients:

- 2 tbsp. of onion, diced
- 1 tbsp. of oil, vegetable + more for frying
- 1 minced clove of garlic, small
- 2 tbsp. of celery, diced
- 1 tsp. of parsley, minced
- 2 cups of plain, dry bread crumbs
- 1 tsp. of mustard, Dijon
- 1 tsp. of minced tarragon, fresh
- 1 dash of tabasco sauce
- A dash of Worcestershire sauce

- 1/2 tsp. of salt, sea
- 1/4 cup of diced bell pepper, yellow or red
- 1 1/4 lbs. of crab meat

Instructions:

1. Add oil, celery and onion to sauté pan on med. heat. Cook for four to five minutes, till they soften. Add the garlic. Cook for a minute more. Transfer mixture to bowl. Allow to cool.

2. Add crab meat, tabasco and Worcestershire sauces, salt, ground pepper, mustard, herbs and one cup of bread crumbs to bowl. Make patties of about 3 1/2 inches in width and 1/2" in thickness.

3. Spread the rest of the bread crumbs on a large plate. Turn crab cakes in crumbs and lightly coat. Set cakes on wire rack. Allow to dry for 15-20 minutes.
4. Heat 1/4" of oil in large sized sauté pan over med-high heat. Add the crab cakes. Don't place too close together. Fry as the cakes crisp and brown, which will take three to four minutes for each side. Transfer to paper towel-lined plate. Serve on greens.

American food, Southern style...

6 – Southern Baked Chicken

The Southern area of America is known for fried chicken too, but this baked chicken has a wonderful taste and it doesn't leave a fried oil smell in your house. It is also lighter, and easier to put together.

Makes 4 Servings
Cooking + Prep Time: 1 3/4 hours

- 1/2 tsp. of garlic powder
- 2 cups of panko breadcrumbs
- Salt, kosher
- Pepper, ground
- 1/4 cup of buttermilk
- 3 eggs, large
- 6 chicken thighs, skin on, bone in

Instructions:

1. Preheat the oven to 425F. Line baking sheet with foil.
2. Mix garlic powder and breadcrumbs together in medium sized bowl. Add salt ground pepper.
3. In a separate bowl, whisk buttermilk and eggs together.

4. Pat the chicken thighs dry. Dip them into the egg mixture and dredge in breadcrumbs. Be sure each side is coated completely. Place on baking sheet. Bake till crispy and golden. This should take about an hour. Remove from oven and serve hot.

7 – Cajun Jambalaya

Jambalaya is like a union between paella and risotto. The rice is creamy, as you'd find in risotto dishes, and the chicken, shrimp and andouille sausage combine to offer a wonderful taste. This dish harkens back to French and Spanish people who settled in the Gulf states of America.

Makes 4 Servings
Cooking + Prep Time: 45 minutes

- 1 chopped onion
- 2 chopped bell peppers
- 1 tbsp. of oil, olive
- Salt, kosher
- Black pepper, ground
- 1 tsp. of oregano, dried
- 1 pound of 1-inch cubed chicken breasts, skinless,

boneless
- 2 minced garlic cloves
- 6 ounces of sliced andouille sausage
- 2 cups of chicken stock, low sodium
- 2 tbsp. of tomato paste
- 1 cup of rice, long grain
- 1 x 15-ounce can of tomatoes, crushed
- 1 pound of de-veined, peeled shrimp, medium
- 2 sliced green onions
- 2 tsp. of Old Bay seasoning

Instructions:

1. Heat the oil in large sized pot on med. heat. Add bell peppers and onion. Season using salt and ground pepper. Cook for three to five minutes, till they are soft. Stir in chicken. Use oregano, salt and ground pepper to season.

2. Cook chicken for three to five minutes, till golden. Stir in tomato paste, andouille sausage and garlic. Cook for a minute or so longer, till they become fragrant.

3. Add the chicken broth, Old Bay seasoning, crushed tomatoes and rice. Lower heat to med-low. Cover. Cook till rice becomes tender and liquid has been almost fully absorbed. This will usually take 15-20 minutes.

4. Add shrimp. Cook till they are pink, three to five minutes. 5. Stir in the green onions and serve.

8 – Blackened Catfish

Blackened fish are juicy and perfectly cooked, and their coating includes tasty herbs and spices. This is a fairly light dish, considering the amount of flavor it packs. One you have tried blackened fish once, you may want to prepare it more often.

Makes 4 Servings
Cooking + Prep Time: 35 minutes
Ingredients:

- 2 cups water, filtered
- 1 cup rice, white
- 1/2 tsp. pepper sauce, hot
- 1 tsp. Cajun seasoning
- 1 tsp. black pepper, ground
- 1/2 tsp. garlic powder
- 1 tsp. thyme, ground

- 1 tsp. salt, sea
- 1/2 tsp. onion powder
- 1 tsp. cayenne pepper, ground
- 1/2 tsp. dill weed, dried
- 1/2 tsp. paprika
- 2 x 8-oz. catfish fillets
- 1/4 tsp. pepper, lemon
- 1 tsp. lemon juice, as desired
- 1/2 cup melted butter

Instructions:

1. Bring water, rice, hot pepper sauce and Cajun seasoning to boil in sauce pan. Reduce the heat to med-low. Cover. Simmer till rice becomes tender and liquid is absorbed. This typically takes between 20 and 25 minutes.

2. As rice cooks, mix the lemon pepper, dill weed, paprika, onion powder, garlic powder, salt, cayenne and black peppers and thyme in medium bowl, till blended well. Brush the fillets with the butter. Sprinkle with the mixture of seasonings on each side.

3. Heat leftover butter in large skillet on med-high. Pan-fry the newly-seasoned catfish in the butter till you can flake it easily using a fork.

4. Pour leftover butter over the catfish. Sprinkle it with lemon juice and serve on rice.

9 – Loaded Grits

This creamy dish will even be appealing to people who don't like grits. Outside of the Southern states, grits are not consumed much. But they make a great comfort food, and this dish works well for breakfast on special days or holidays.

Makes 6-8 Servings
Cooking + Prep Time: 30 minutes + 3 hours slow cooker time
Ingredients:

- 6 cups of water, filtered
- 1 1/2 cup of grits
- 1 1/2 cup of cheddar cheese shreds
- 6 slices of cooked, crumbled bacon
- Salt, kosher
- Black pepper, ground

- 3 sliced green onions
- 2 tbsp. of butter, unsalted

Instructions:

1. In bowl of your slow cooker, combine the water, grits, 3 slices of bacon and 1 cup of cheese shreds. Season using kosher salt and ground pepper. Allow mixture to sit for just a minute or so, allowing grits to settle.

2. Cover. Cook over high heat till grits become tender. Stir occasionally for 2 1/2 to 3 hours.

3. Add remaining bacon and cheese, butter and green onions. Stir till butter has melted and serve warm.

10 – Southern Style Biscuits Gravy

There is nothing quite like the down-home comfort food of biscuits and gravy. They make a wonderful breakfast, paired with fruit, or with eggs for a larger meal. You can serve them at brunch time, too.

Makes 6-8 Servings
Cooking + Prep Time: 1 hour
Ingredients:

- 3 tbsp. of flour, all-purpose
- 1 pound of sausage, Italian, with removed casings
- A pinch of cayenne pepper
- 2 1/2 cups of milk, whole
- Salt, kosher
- Ground pepper, black
- 2 tbsp. of melted butter, unsalted

- 1 can of biscuits, each cut in quarters
- 1 tbsp. of chopped chives

Instructions:

1. Preheat the oven to 375F. Spray large casserole dish with non-stick spray.

2. In large sized skillet on med., cook the sausage till it is browned. Drain, as desired. Sprinkle flour over sausage. Cook a minute longer. Season with salt, cracked pepper and cayenne.

3. Pour milk over mixture. Bring it to boil and whisk to fully combine. Lower heat. Simmer till it is thick, and remove pan from heat.

4. Place 1/2 of quartered biscuits on bottom of casserole dish. Pour gravy mixture over them. Top with rest of biscuits. Brush them with the butter.
5. Place casserole dish in oven. Bake for 15-18 minutes, till sausage mixture bubbles and biscuits become golden. Use chives to garnish. Serve.

Midwestern recipes– from the heart of America

11 – Chicago Deep Dish Pizza

You don't have to fly to Chicago to taste their traditional pizza– you can make them at home! These pizzas have a flaky, thick crust, rich sauce and lots of cheese– just like they make them in the city of broad shoulders.

Makes 2 pizza pies, 8 servings each
Cooking + Prep Time: 1 1/2 hours
Ingredients:

- 1/4 cup of corn meal
- 3 1/2 cups of flour, all-purpose
- 1 1/2 tsp. of sugar, granulated
- 1/4 oz. of yeast, quick rise
- 1 cup of water, filtered
- 1/3 cup of oil, olive
- 1/2 tsp. of salt, kosher

Toppings

- 1 x 28-oz. can of drained tomatoes, diced
- 6 cups of mozzarella cheese shreds
- 1 x 8-oz. can of tomato paste
- 1 x 8-oz. can of tomato sauce
- 1/2 tsp. of salt, kosher
- 1/4 tsp. each of ground pepper, basil, oregano and garlic powder
- 48 slices of pepperoni
- 1 lb. of cooked, crumbled Italian sausage, mild
- 1/4 cup of Parmesan cheese, grated
- 1/2 lb. of sliced mushrooms, fresh

Instructions:

1. Combine corn meal, 1 1/2 cups of all-purpose flour, yeast, salt and sugar in large sized bowl.

2. Heat oil and water up to 120 to 130F in sauce pan. Add this to the dry ingredients and beat only until it has moistened. Add the rest of the flour to form your dough.

3. Turn the dough onto floured cutting board. Knead it till elastic and smooth. Place in greased medium bowl. Turn once to grease the top.

4. Cover bowl. Allow dough to rise in warm part of house until size doubles. This usually takes about 1/2 hour.

5. Punch the dough down and divide it in halves. Roll both portions into 11" circles. Press dough onto bottom and up sides of two pre-greased ovenproof skillets. Sprinkle with 2 cups of mozzarella cheese each.

6. Combine tomato paste, tomato sauce and tomatoes with seasonings in large sized bowl. Spoon 1 1/2 cups of this mixture over each of the pizzas.

7. Layer pizzas with mushrooms, sausage and pepperoni. Add 1 cup of mozzarella cheese and 2 tbsp. of Parmesan cheese each.

8. Cover skillets. Bake for 30-35 minutes at 450F. Remove lids from skillets. Bake for five more minutes until the dough has browned lightly. Serve.

12 – Kansas City Bbq Ribs

The ribs in Kansas City are prepared in sticky, thick sauce that brings the other tastes together in a wonderful way. The sweetness of brown sugar is tempered by the hotter spices. Theyare indeed worthy of licking one's fingers.

Makes 12 Servings
Cooking + Prep Time: 1 3/4 hours
Ingredients:

• 2 tsp. each of smoke paprika, garlic powder and onion powder
• 1 1/3 cups of brown sugar, packed
• 12 pork ribs, country-style, bone-in
• 1 1/4 tsp. each of cayenne pepper, ground cumin and ground black pepper

For the sauce

- 1 chopped onion, medium
- 2 tbsp. of oil, canola
- 1/3 cup of brown sugar, dark
- 1 cup of tomato sauce
- 1/4 cup of molasses
- 1/4 cup of ketchup
- 2 tbsp. of Worcestershire sauce
- 1 tbsp. of vinegar, apple cider
- 1 tsp. of mustard, ground
- 1 tsp. of salt, kosher
- 1/4 tsp. pf pepper, cayenne
- 1/4 tsp. of paprika, smoked

Instructions:

1. Mix the brown sugar along with seasonings in small sized bowl. Sprinkle it over the ribs. Cover and refrigerate for an hour or more.
2. To create the sauce, heat the oil on med. heat in large sized sauce pan. Add the onion. Stir and cook till tender, about five or six minutes. Stir in the remainder of ingredients and bring to boil. Stir occasionally and remove pan from heat.

3. Wrap the ribs in foil and seal the edges. Cover and grill on indirect med. heat for 1 1/4 – 1 3/4 hours. Ribs should be tender.

4. Remove ribs carefully from the foil. Place ribs on med. heat. Baste with some sauce. Cover and grill for eight to 10 minutes, till browned. Turn and baste occasionally while grilling, with the rest of the sauce. Serve.

13 – Chili, Cincinnati Slow Cooker Style

I like trying new dishes, but I still have some that my family asks for all the time. This is one of them. It's a Midwest comfort food, and it may be one you'll be making often.

Makes   10   Servings
Cooking + Prep Time: 1/2 hour + 5 hours slow cooker time
Ingredients:

- 1 1/2 cups of onions, chopped
- 3 lbs. of beef, ground
- 2 x 16-oz. cans of rinsed drained kidney beans
- 1 1/2 tsp. of garlic, minced
- 2 cups of broth, beef
- 2 x 15-oz. cans of tomato sauce
- 1 oz. of chopped chocolate, unsweetened
- 1/4 cup each of Worcestershire sauce, red wine

vinegar and chili powder
- 1 1/2 tsp. each of ground cumin and ground cinnamon
- 1 tsp. of oregano, dried
- 1 tsp. of salt, kosher
- 1/8 tsp. of cloves, ground
- Spaghetti, cooked, hot
- 1/2 tsp. of pepper, black, ground

Optional: sliced green onions and cheddar cheese shreds

Instructions:

1. Cook the onions and beef in large skillet on med. heat till meat is not pink any longer. Add the garlic and cook for a minute more. Drain.

2. In slow cooker, combine tomato sauce, beans, chili powder, broth, Worcestershire sauce, vinegar, cinnamon, chocolate, cloves, pepper, oregano, salt and cumin.

3. Cover. Cook on low setting for five to six hours till mixture is heated completely through.
4. Garnish with green onions and cheese, as desired. Serve with spaghetti.

14 – Midwest Meat Loaf

This is classic meat loaf that is made the original way, with a catsup glaze on top. You'll find this to be a great recipe for ground beef.

Makes 6 Servings
Cooking + Prep Time: 1 hour 40 minutes
Ingredients:

- 1/3 cup of milk, evaporated
- 1 lightly beaten egg, large
- 3/4 cup of oats, quick cooking
- 2 tbsp. of Worcestershire sauce
- 1 tsp. of salt, kosher
- 1/4 cup of onion, chopped
- 1/8 tsp. of pepper, ground
- 1 1/2 lbs. of beef, ground
- 1/2 tsp. of sage, rubbed
- 1/4 cup of catsup

Instructions:

1. Combine milk, egg, Worcestershire sauce, pepper, sage, salt, onion and oats in large sized bowl. Crumble the beef over this mixture. Combine well.

2. Press into 4" x 8" loaf pan. Leave uncovered and bake for 1 1/4 hours at 350F. Then drain.

3. Spread catsup over the meatloaf. Bake for 10 more minutes till meat shows no more pink. Internal temp. should be 160F. Allow to stand for 8-10 minutes. Slice and serve.

15 – Pork Tenderloin

This recipe has been in my regular rotation for years. It requires only minimal effort, and you'll be amazed at the flavor the first time you try it.

Makes 4 Servings
Cooking + Prep Time: 35 minutes
Ingredients:

- 1/3 cup of flour, all-purpose
- 1 lb. of pork tenderloin
- 1/2 tsp. of salt, kosher
- 1/3 cup of muffin or corn bread mix
- 1 beaten egg, large
- 4 tbsp. of oil, canola
- 1/4 tsp. of pepper, ground

Optional: BBQ sauce or ranch sauce
Instructions:

1. Cut the pork crossways into slices of 1/2" each.
2. Mix the flour, salt, ground pepper and corn bread mix in shallow, large bowl.
3. Place the egg in separate, medium shallow bowl.
4. Dip the pork in the egg, then in the flour mixture. Pat so the coating will adhere better.

5. Heat 2 tbsp. of oil on med. heat in large sized skillet. Add
1/2 of pork. Cook it for three to four minutes per side. Drain pork on plate lined with paper towels.

6. Wipe the skillet clean. Repeat steps with the rest of the pork and oil. Serve with sauce, as desired.

Recipes From The Historic American Southwest...

16 – Black Bean Soup

What a simple recipe this is, and it still fills you up! I use fresh tomatoes when they're in season, but the canned tomatoes fill in OK if that's all that is available to you when they aren't in season.

Makes 6 **Servings**
Cooking + Prep Time: 35 minutes
Ingredients:

- 2 tsp. of garlic, minced
- 3 x 15-oz. cans of undrained black beans
- 1/2 tsp. of pepper flakes, red
- 1/2 tbsp. of chili powder
- 1 tsp. of cumin, ground

- 1 tsp. of salt, kosher
- 1/2 tsp. of chili pepper, chipotle
- 1 x 10-oz. can of tomatoes with chilies
- 1 x 11-oz. can of drained yellow corn
- 14 oz. of broth, vegetable

Instructions:

1. Empty a can of black beans in food processor. Add the salt, cumin, chipotle chili pepper, red pepper flakes, chili powder and garlic. Cover. Blend for about 1/2 minute and pour the mixture into a stock pot.

2. Stir the remaining two cans of black beans into stock pot, along with corn, broth and tomatoes. Bring to boil, then lower the heat to med. Simmer for 20-25 minutes and serve.

17 – Southwestern Chicken Quesadillas

Quesadillas are quite popular in my house, especially since they are an easy meal to grab on the go. As long as you have cheese, you can usually find enough other ingredients in your fridge to flesh out the recipe.

Makes 8 Servings (2 wedges each)
Cooking + Prep Time: 55 minutes + 6 hours of marinating time
Ingredients:

- 3/4 cup of thawed lime juice concentrate
- 4 chicken breast halves, skinless, boneless
- 1 sliced onion, large
- 2 julienned sweet peppers, one yellow and one orange
- 1/4 tsp. of salt, kosher
- 1 tbsp. of oil, canola

- 1/4 tsp. of pepper, ground black
- 4 x 10" tortillas, flour
- 1 cup of cheddar cheese shreds
- 1 cup of Monterey Jack cheese shreds
- 1 tbsp. of lime juice
- 2 tbsp. of melted butter
- 1 tbsp. of cilantro, chopped

Optional: lime wedges

Instructions:

1. Place the chicken in large sized bowl. Add the concentrated limeade. Toss and coat. Cover the bowl and refrigerate for at least six hours, or overnight.

2. Sauté peppers and onion in oil in large skillet till they are tender. Season them with kosher salt and ground pepper. Remove them and set them aside. Wipe the skillet out. Drain the chicken. Discard marinade.

3. Cover the chicken and grill on greased rack on med. heat for five to eight minutes per side. Cut the chicken into 1/4" strips. Set them aside.

4. On 1/2 of tortillas, layer Monterey Jack shreds, chicken, onion mixture and cheddar shreds. Fold them over. Combine lime juice and butter and brush tortillas with it.

5. In the skillet you previously used for veggies, cook the quesadillas on med. heat till the cheese melts. Keep each warm in the oven while you cook the remaining ones.

6. Cut quesadillas into 4 wedges each. Sprinkle them with cilantro and serve with the lime wedges, as desired.

18 – Lasagna, Tex Mex Style

This recipe packs great taste, and it's easy to make, as well. You can add extra cheese if you like– it adds protein as well as flavor. If you have leftovers (don't count on it), they can be frozen for later.

Makes 6-8 **Servings**
Cooking + Prep Time: 1 1/2 hours
Ingredients:
For sauce

- 3 cups of water, filtered
- 2 x 8-oz. cans of tomato sauce
- 3 tbsp. of chili powder
- 4 tbsp. of corn starch
- 1/4 tsp. of garlic powder
- 1/2 tsp. of onion powder

To assemble

- 4 cups pinto beans, mashed, cooked
- 12 tortillas, corn
- 1 1/2 cups of frozen and thawed corn
- 1 x 2 1/4 oz. can of drained ripe olives, sliced
- 1 cup of green onions, chopped

Optional: Salsa and 1 to 2 tbsp. of green chilies, chopped

Instructions:

1. To create the sauce, place its ingredients in sauce pan.

Whisk till combined well. Stir while cooking on med. heat till it thickens. Taste. Add additional chili powder, to taste. Set the sauce aside.

2. Place beans in large sized bowl. Add olives, corn and onions + green chilies, as desired. Combine till mixed well. Set the bowl aside.

3. Preheat your oven to 350F.
4. Place 1 1/2 cups of sauce in nonstick 13" x 9" casserole dish.
5. Place 4 of the corn tortillas across the bottom. It's ok if they overlap.

6. Spread 1/2 bean mixture on tortillas. Place four more tortillas over bean mixture. Spread the rest of the bean mixture on top of second tortilla layer.

7. Cover beans with baking paper and foil. Crimp edges around the casserole dish.
8. Bake dish for 40-45 minutes. Remove it from oven. Allow to sit for 10-15 minutes. Serve.

19 – Southwest Rice Vegetable Casserole

The rice in this dish gives it the flavorful base upon which you can build dinner. There are tons of vegetables, for fiber, and cheddar cheese adds a final tasty treat.

Makes 8 Servings
Cooking + Prep Time: 1 1/4 hours
Ingredients:

- 1 diced onion, medium
- 2 tbsp. of oil, vegetable
- 1 de-seeded, diced jalapeño, medium
- 2 minced garlic cloves
- 1 quartered, sliced zucchini, medium
- 1 de-seeded, diced bell pepper, medium
- 3/4 tsp. of salt, kosher

- 1/2 tbsp. of chili powder
- 1 x 15-oz. can of tomatoes, diced, with chilies
- 1 cup of corn kernels, frozen
- 3 cups of rice
- 1 x 15-oz. can of drained, rinsed black beans
- 2 sliced green onions
- 2 cups of sharp cheddar cheese shreds

Instructions:
1. Preheat oven to 375F. Coat 8" x 8" baking dish with cooking spray.

2. In large sized skillet on med-low, heat oil. Add garlic and onion. Stir till onions soften. Add bell pepper, jalapeño pepper, salt, zucchini and chili powder to skillet. Combine by stirring.

3. Increase heat to med. Continue sautéing till veggies are soft and there is no remaining liquid in skillet.

4. Combine black beans, diced chilies and tomatoes and corn in large sized bowl. Add sautéed veggies, cheddar and rice to bowl. Sir till mixed evenly.

5. Pour veggie and rice mixture into baking dish, Bake for
 18-20 minutes. Sprinkle green onions over the top of casserole. Serve.

20 – Pork Chile Posole

This spicy stew is a traditional dish in the areas around the state of New Mexico. The pork and chilies come together and warm you up. You can serve it with cornbread or tortillas, if you like.

Makes 2 Servings
Cooking + Prep Time: 1 1/4 hours
Ingredients:

- 1/2 cup of onion, diced
- 1 1/4 tsp. of oil, olive
- 2 tbsp. of cilantro, chopped
- 1/4 cup of celery, diced
- 1/2 lb. of diced pork loin, boneless, lean
- 2 1/2 tsp. of garlic, chopped
- 1/2 cup of green poblano pepper, diced
- 1/2 cup of canned corn, drained

- 2 tsp. of cumin seeds
- 3 oz. of diced tomatillos, canned
- 2 3/4 cups of stock, chicken
- 2 tsp. of chili powder, dark
- Kosher salt and ground pepper

Optional: 1 tsp. of coriander, ground
Instructions:

1. Heat the oil in large sized pan on med-high. Sauté garlic,
1 tbsp. of cilantro, celery and onion till the onion has softened.

2. Add the pork. Cook while stirring till meat has browned on outside. Add corn, stock, chili powder, cumin, tomatillos, poblanos and the coriander, as desired. Use kosher salt and ground pepper to season.
3. Cover the pan. Simmer till pork is white and tender. Add remaining tbsp. of cilantro and stir. Serve.

Favorite Recipes Of The American Pacific Northwest

21 – Smoked Salmon Scramble

Picture a soft pile of scrambled eggs, topped with cheese and salmon, with a fewscattered green onion pieces on top. It's a great recipe to share with family and friends alike.

Makes 4-6 Servings
Cooking + Prep Time: 25 minutes
Ingredients:

- Salt, kosher
- Pepper, ground, black

- 8 eggs, large
- 8 oz. of flaked, smoked salmon, wild
- 3/4 cup of butter, unsalted
- 5 oz. of goat cheese, soft, creamy
- 2 halved lengthways, sliced green onions, large
- • grain bread, toasted, sliced in 1/2" slices
- 2 tbsp. of honey, pure

Instructions:

1. Whisk eggs together till they are smooth. Season with kosher salt and ground pepper. Melt 1/4 cup of butter in large sauté pan on med. heat till it starts simmering.

2. Add eggs. Cook them slowly on low heat till they form soft mounds. Add 3/4 of salmon plus green onions and stir well. Fold mixture one last time. Remove from heat.

3. Spoon mixture on serving platter. Garnish with the rest of the salmon.

4. Stir honey, remaining butter and goat cheese together. Season using kosher salt ground pepper. Spread over justwarmed toast. Serve with eggs.

22 – Northwest Prawn Spinach Pasta

This tasty one-dish recipe is a delight for the senses. You can serve it for guests, or for the family. You may use either ricotta or goat cheese- they both taste great.

Makes 4 **Servings**
Cooking + Prep Time: 1/2 hour
Ingredients:

- 2 tbsp. of vinegar, balsamic
- 2 tbsp. of oil, olive
- 1/2 tsp. of salt, kosher
- 3 tbsp. of chopped basil, fresh
- 1/4 tsp. of black pepper, ground
- 3 cups of pasta, penne
- 3 minced cloves of garlic
- 1 tbsp. of oil, olive
- 4 chopped tomatoes, Roma

- 12 oz. of de-veined, peeled shrimp, large
- 3/4 cup of crumbled ricotta cheese
- 2 cups of spinach leaves, packed
- 2 tbsp. of Parmesan cheese shavings

Instructions:

1. Combine the first 5 ingredients in large sized bowl and set it aside.
2. Cook pasta in large pot of salted, boiling water till they are firm but tender.
3. Add in olive oil mixture and cover. Keep warm.

4. Heat 1 tbsp. of oil on med-high. Add garlic. Cook for a minute. Add the prawns. Cook and stir occasionally for about five minutes.
5. Add the spinach, tomatoes and cooked pasta. Toss over heat till spinach wilts.

6. Sprinkle with parmesan and ricotta. Fold gently in. Serve promptly.

23 – Pacific Razor Clam Chowder

The Pacific Northwest has abundant seafood. One of the most unique is the razor clam. This recipe for clam chowder tastes worlds away from the East Coast clam chowder above, but they are just on opposite ends of America.

Makes 8 Servings
Cooking + Prep Time: 1 hour 10 minutes
Ingredients:

- 6 chopped red potatoes, small
- 15 fresh-caught razor clams
- 3 chopped shallots
- 1/2 pound of sliced bacon, Applewood smoked
- 4 minced garlic cloves
- 5 chopped stalks of celery, leaves included
- 1/4 cup of butter, unsalted

- 5 cups of milk, whole
- 1 x 8-ounce brick cream cheese, reduced fat
- 2 tbsp. of chopped Italian parsley
- 2 tsp. of thyme leaves, fresh
- 2 dashes of tabasco sauce
- 1 tbsp. of minced chives
- 1/4 cup of potato flakes, instant
- 1 pinch each red pepper flakes, Himalayan pink sea salt and black pepper, ground

Optional: 1/2 pint of cream, heavy

Instructions:

1. To large sized sauce pan, add milk, clams with any juice, pepper flakes, tabasco sauce, parsley, thyme, heavy cream (as desired), butter and cream cheese. Gently heat on low.

2. In skillet, render bacon till almost crisp. Add garlic, shallot, celery and potatoes. Fry till the potatoes are nearly tender. Add this mixture to the clam and milk mixture.

3. Slowly heat on low till potatoes are fully tender.

4. Add potato flakes, 1 tbsp. after another, till chowder has reached your desired thickness. Season using pink sea salt and ground pepper, as desired. Use chopped chives to garnish. Serve hot.

24 – Raspberry Arugula Salmon

This is a great blend of flavors that has been made for more years than you might think. It's a step up from routine salads and salmon dishes, and the blend of salmon and raspberries is delightful.

Makes 4 Servings
Cooking + Prep Time: 50 minutes + 2 hours refrigeration time
Ingredients:

- 8 crushed raspberries
- 1/2 cup of softened butter, unsalted
- 1 tsp. of salt, kosher
- 2 tbsp. of baby arugula, minced finely
- 3 tbsp. of oil, olive
- 3/8 tsp. of black pepper, ground
- For the dressing
- 8 more crushed raspberries

- 2 tsp. of vinegar, raspberry
- 4 x 6-oz. salmon fillets, pin bones and skin removed

To garnish: fresh raspberries, baby arugula leaves

Instructions:

1. Blend 8 crushed raspberries, arugula, butter, 1/2 tsp. of kosher salt 1/8 tsp. of ground pepper with fork in small sized bowl.

2. Spoon this mixture onto wax paper sheet. Form into 4" long log. Twist wax paper ends to seal. Place in fridge for an hour or longer.

3. Stir second 8 crushed raspberries, olive oil, raspberry vinegar, 1/2 tsp. of kosher salt and 1/4 tsp. of ground pepper in shallow dish.

4. Add salmon to dish. Cover. Marinate in the fridge for minimum of one hour, maximum of four hours.

5. Remove the salmon from its marinade. Discard remaining marinade. Grill the salmon on med-high for three to five minutes per side. Place 2 pats raspberry-arugula log on fillets. Allow them to melt over the fish. Add garnish, as desired. Serve.

25 – Baked Oysters

These succulent oysters are brightened by hazelnuts and leeks, making a wonderful choice for a dinner with guests. You can cook more oysters and use the dish as your main course, too.

Makes 6-8 Servings
Cooking + Prep Time: 1 hour 50 minutes
Ingredients:

- 2 cups of leeks, sliced
- 1 tbsp. of oil, olive
- 1/4 cup of vermouth, dry
- 1/2 cup of toasted hazelnuts, chopped
- 1/4 tsp. of salt, kosher
- 1/8 tsp. of pepper, ground

- 2 tbsp. of parsley, chopped
- 24 oysters in shell, medium sized

Instructions:

1. Cut piece of aluminum foil 2x as long as cookie sheet. Crumple foil loosely and line cookie sheet with it. Set it aside.

2. Heat oil in large sized skillet on med-high. Add the leeks. Cook for four minutes while stirring. They should begin softening.

3. Cover pan. Lower heat to med. Cook for eight minutes while stirring, till the leeks become tender.

4. Remove the pan from the heat. Stir in hazelnuts, vermouth, parsley, kosher salt and ground pepper.

5. Scrub the oyster shells. Shuck them and discard tops. Arrange oyster bottoms on the crumbled foil in cookie sheet. The foil will keep the oysters from falling over. Top the oysters with the leek mixture.

6. Bake in batches at 475F, till oysters become plump and their edges bubble. Arrange carefully on platter. Serve promptly.

Authentic Recipes of Native Americans

26 – Hopi Stew With Dumplings

This recipe comes from Arizona, from the native tribal lands of the Hopi Indians. It's actually easy to make with canned foods, and it's hearty and spicy.

Makes 4-6 Servings
Cooking + Prep Time: 1 3/4 hours
Ingredients:
For stew

- 1 1/2 pounds of beef, ground
- 2 tbsp. of bacon drippings
- 1 chopped bell pepper, green
- 1 chopped onion, medium
- 4 cups of corn kernels
- 1 tbsp. of New Mexico ground red pepper
- 1 small squash, yellow
- 1 zucchini, small
- 1 tbsp. of flour, whole wheat

- 4 cups of water, filtered
- Salt, kosher, as desired

For dumplings

- 2 tsp. of baking powder
- 2 cups of corn meal, blue
- 1/2 tsp. of salt, kosher
- 2 tbsp. of bacon drippings
- 2/3 cup of milk, whole

Instructions:

1. To create the stew, heat the bacon drippings on med-high in large sized pot. Add meat. Sauté till browned lightly. Stir in ground chili, onion and pepper. Sauté till the onion becomes translucent.
2. Add squash, corn and zucchini and water to cover them. Stir well. Bring to boil. Reduce heat to med-low. Simmer for 30 to 40 minutes. Veggies and meat should be tender.

3. Combine 2 tbsp. broth from stew and the flour in small sized bowl. Whisk the mixture back into stew. Simmer till it thickens. Add dumplings in last 15 minutes.

4. To create the dumplings, mix salt, bacon drippings, baking powder and corn meal in medium bowl. Add

milk to make batter stiff. Drop tbsp-fulls into stew in last 15 minutes of its cooking. Remove from heat. Stir.

27 – Seminole Fried Tomatoes

This is an adaptable recipe from the Seminole tribe that you'll probably like a lot. Adding cayenne pepper will spice it up, if you like some heat. The tomato slices hold the batter well, and it's quite a filling dish.

Makes 4-6 Servings
Cooking + Prep Time: 45 minutes
Ingredients:

- 1 tsp. of salt, kosher
- 4 green tomatoes, large
- 2 cups of corn meal, yellow, ground
- Vegetable shortening
- A pinch of ground pepper

Instructions:

1. Slice the tomatoes to 1/2" thickness. Sprinkle with kosher salt. Allow to stand for 8-15 minutes. Then blot them dry using paper towels. Sprinkle them with pepper.

2. Dip tomato slices in corn meal.
3. Heat shortening in large skillet till it starts smoking. Fry tomato slices till both sides are brown. Serve promptly.

28 – Sisters Stew

The "sisters" in this recipe are not relatives in anyone's family, but rather corn, squash and beans, which are known by Native Americans as the "three sisters" of food.

Makes 4 Servings
Cooking + Prep Time: 55 minutes
Ingredients:

- 2 to 2 1/2 cups of rinsed mushrooms, chopped
- 1 to 1 1/2 cups of kidney beans, cooked
- 2 to 2 1/2 cups of yellow squash, cut
- 1 to 1 1/2 cups of defrosted from frozen kernels of

corn
- 1 diced potato, large
- 1 x 16-oz. can of drained tomatoes, diced
- 1/2 tsp. of ground pepper, black

- 1 diced onion, large
- 1/4 tsp. of thyme
- 1/2 tsp. of sage
- 1/2 tsp. of cilantro
- 1/4 tsp. of salt, kosher
- 1/2 tsp. of rosemary
- 2 to 4 bay leaves
- 2 to 3 minced cloves of garlic
- 1 tbsp. of oil, olive

Instructions:
1. Heat oil, 1/2 of spices and garlic in large sized pot. Sauté onions for two to four minutes.
2. Add 2 to 4 cups of filtered water. Allow mixture to come to boil.

3. Add potatoes and second 1/2 of spices and simmer for three to five minutes.
4. Add beans, corn and tomatoes. Allow to simmer for three to five minutes.

5. Add mushrooms and squash. Allow to simmer for 12 minutes to 1/2 hour, until the mixture is cooked to your preference. Serve.

29 – Cherokee Beef Pepperpot Soup

This recipe can be made with various meats, like beef shanks or short ribs, or venison. The tomatoes, turnips, peppers and other veggies make the dish appealing and filling, too.

Makes 8-10 Servings
Cooking + Prep Time: 3 hours 55 minutes
Ingredients:

- 1 quart of water, filtered
- 1 pound of beef short ribs
- 3 peeled, chopped tomatoes, ripe
- 2 quartered onions, large
- 1 peeled, cubed turnip, large
- 1 seeded, diced bell pepper, sweet
- 1/2 cup of sliced carrot
- 1/2 cup of diced potatoes
- 1/4 cup of minced celery

- 1/2 cup of corn kernels
- Salt, kosher
- Black pepper, ground

Instructions:

1. Place meat in large pot. Cover with filtered water till water is one inch higher than meat. Cover. Bring to boil on high heat.

2. Reduce the heat. Simmer for two and one-half hours.
3. Remove the meat and let it cool.
4. Discard the bones and return meat to pot.
5. Add all veggies. Cover. Simmer for one to one and a half hours.
6. Season as desired and serve.

30 – Navajo Chili

This is SUCH an easy chili recipe. It is a crowd-pleaser, as chili often is. You can use tomatoes from your own garden for the most enjoyable flavor, but you can also use storebought or canned, to make the recipe easier.

Makes 8 **Servings**
Cooking + Prep Time: 1 hour 45 minutes
Ingredients:

- 3 cups of water, boiling
- 1 large chili, ancho
- 3 tbsp. of oil, olive
- 1/4 cup of dried mushrooms, porcini
- Salt, kosher
- Black pepper, ground
- 2 lbs. of beef chuck or ground buffalo meat
- 4 minced cloves of garlic, large
- 2 chopped onions, large

- 1/4 cup of water mixed with 2 tbsp. of tomato paste
- 2 tbsp. of chili powder, pure
- 1 cup of stock, chicken

Instructions:

1. Using an oven-safe bowl, cover ancho chilies with 2 cups boiling water. Place porcini in small bowl. Cover with other 1 cup boiling water. Allow both to soak until they have softened. This will take 20-30 minutes.

2. Remove ancho and discard seeds and stem. Chop finely. Reserve soaking liquid. Rub porcini, removing grit, if any. Chop finely. Reserve their soaking liquid.

3. In large casserole, heat 2 tbsp. of oil till nearly smoking.

4. Add 1/2 of ground meat in one layer. Season using kosher salt ground pepper. Sear meat on high heat for three minutes.

5. Stir meat gently and continue browning for two more minutes. Use a slotted spoon to transfer meat to plate. Brown the rest of the meat.

6. Heat remaining oil in casserole. Add onions. Cook on low till they become soft. Add garlic and stir while cooking till it is fragrant.

7. Add chili powder. Stir and cook for four to five minutes. Add tomato paste mixture, porcini, chicken stock and ancho. Season with large pinch salt. Simmer on med-low till sauce has been reduced by 1/3.

8. Stir in meat gently. Bring to temperature of mixture in pot. Serve hot.

Connecticut - White Clam Pizza

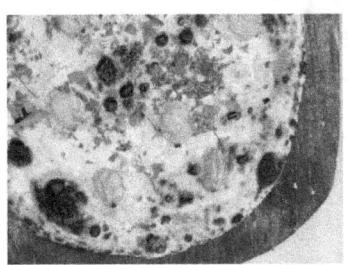

Connecticut's white clam pizza combines the saltiness of clams with the creaminess of mozzarella and the nuttiness of Parmesan.

This pizza was introduced to New Haven by Francis Roselli who, after WW1 having come to the US from southern Italy, began making pizzas in his bakery.

Francis first began selling tomato pies and then local clams before finally deciding to make a clam pizza. The rest, as they say, is history.

Portions: 4-6

Prep Time: 25mins

Total Time: 2hours 10mins

Ingredients:

Dough:

- ¾ cup water (110 to 115 degrees F)
- 1½ tsp active dry yeast
- 1 teaspoon sugar
- 2¼ cups all-purpose flour + additional for kneading
- 1 tsp kosher salt
- 2 tbsp. olive oil + more for oiling

Topping:

- ¾ cup fresh clams (chopped)
- ¼ cup virgin olive oil + more for drizzling
- 1 tsp dried oregano
- 4 cloves garlic (minced)
- 2 tbsp. cornmeal (for dusting)
- ¾ cup mozzarella (shredded)
- ½ cup Parmesan (grated)
- Kosher salt
- 1 tbsp. parsley (chopped)
- Crushed red pepper (to garnish)

Directions:

1. In a mixing bowl add the warm water, to the yeast and sugar and whisk. Set to one side for 8-10 minutes, or until the yeast activates and starts to become foamy.

2. In a larger mixing bowl, whisk 2¼ cups of flour along with 1 teaspoon of kosher salt. Make a well in the middle of the mixture.

3. Pour the foamy yeast along with 2 tablespoons of olive oil into the well.

4. Turn the dough onto a clean, lightly floured work surface, kneading until smooth; this will take around 5 minutes.

5. Transfer the dough to a lightly oiled mixing bowl and cover with plastic wrap. Place the bowl in a warm place for a couple of hours, or until it becomes twice the size.

6. Meanwhile, drain the clams, setting aside 2 tablespoons of liquid.

7. In a medium bowl, combine the chopped clams along with their juice together with ¼ cup olive oil, oregano, and garlic. Mix well and transfer to the fridge until you are ready.

8. Preheat the main oven to 500 degrees F and place the oven rack on the bottom shelf.

9. Put a pizza stone on the oven rack.

10. As soon as the dough is twice its original size, turn it out onto a lightly floured work surface and carefully stretch it into a rectangular shape of 12x14".

11. Using the cornmeal, lightly dust a pizza paddle and place the dough on top, making sure that it can slide back and forth easily.

12. Sprinkle the mozzarella over the dough.

13. Evenly top with the clam mixture and grated Parmesan.

14. Season with salt.

15. Slide the dough onto the hot pizza stone and cook until the top and underside are golden, for 8-10 minutes.

16. Scatter parsley and crushed pepper over the top and drizzle with oil.

17. Serve!

Delaware - Boiled Crabs In Garlic Butter

In Delaware, the blue crab is of great importance, playing an important role in the state's culture and economy. Great pride is taken in the food that each fisherman provides for the table.

Portions: 6

Prep Time: 15mins
Total Time: 43mins

Ingredients:

- 6 blue crabs
- 2 tbsp. Old Bay seasoning
- Sea salt
- 1 cup butter

- ½ cup fresh garlic (chopped)
- 1 cup parsley leave (chopped)

Directions:

1. Using a large deep pan or pot, fitted with a basket, boil the 6 crabs in sufficient boiling water to completely cover them.

2. Add the Old Bay seasoning and season with sea salt.

3. Boil the crabs for 10 minutes, or until they turn red. Allow the crabs to cool until they are easy to handle.

4. Crack the crabs, and remove lungs, leaving the claws and roe still attached.

5. Crack each crab into two sections, down the center.

6. In a deep sided pan or skillet, melt 1 cup butter and add the chopped garlic and chopped parsley.

7. Arrange the crabs in the butter-garlic mixture and transfer to a large platter.

8. Pour over any butter remaining in the skillet and serve.

Florida - Honey And Orange Glazed Grouper

Oranges play a significant role in the Sunshine State's economy and not surprisingly it is the official state fruit. It's the state beverage, and Florida's state flower is the orange blossom.

This fish recipe is the perfect example of just how versatile this vibrant citrus fruit is.

Portions: 2

Prep Time: 5mins
Total Time: 15mins

Ingredients:

- 1 tbsp. honey

- 1 tbsp. orange marmalade
- 1 tbsp. Florida orange juice
- ¾ tsp Dijon mustard
- ½ tsp light soy sauce
- ⅛ tsp ground white pepper
- ¾ pound grouper fillets

Directions:

1. Preheat the broiler.

2. In a bowl, combine the first 6 ingredients (honey through white pepper) and mix to incorporate.

3. Arrange the grouper on an oiled broiler pan and brush, all over, with the honey glaze.

4. Broil 5-6" away from heat source until browned; this will take 4-5 minutes.

5. Flip the fillets over, brush with glaze, and broil for a further 4-5 minutes or until the fish flakes easily when using a fork.

Georgia - Brown Sugar Pork Chops

With Peach Bbq Sauce

Everything in Georgia is just peachy! Not only did the state designate the peach as its state fruit but a peach features on the US Mint's Georgia quarter. The Peach State produces high-quality fruit which features in lots of recipes and dishes.

Sticky and sweet BBQ pork chops are a perfect way to showcase this fruit's versatility.

Portions: 4

Prep Time: 15mins

Total Time: 1hour 30mins

Ingredients:

- 2 tbsp. canola oil
- 1 sweet onion (finely chopped)
- 1 garlic clove (finely chopped)
- 1 (1") piece fresh ginger (peeled, grated)
- 1½ cups ketchup
- ½ cups peach jam
- 2 ripe peaches (pitted, cut into ¾" chunks)
- 2 tbsp. apple cider vinegar
- Coarse kosher salt and black pepper
- 2 cups water (boiling)
- ¾ cup dark brown sugar
- ¼ cup kosher salt
- 3 cups ice cubes
- 4 (1½ -2 pounds) bone-in pork loin chops

Directions:

1. Over moderate heat in a medium-sized sauté pan, heat the oil.

2. Add the onion and cook for 2 minutes, or until translucent. Add the garlic along with the ginger and cook for 45-60 seconds, until fragrant.

3. Add the ketchup along with the peach jam and chunks of peaches.

4. Reduce the heat and simmer on low until the sauce begins to thicken, occasionally stirring, for 25-30 minutes.

5. Next, add the cider vinegar and season with kosher salt and black pepper.

6. Remove the pan from the heat and put to one side to cool.

7. In the meantime, in a heatproof bowl, and in boiling water, dissolve the brown sugar along with the kosher salt. Stir in the ice cubes to cool.

8. Add the chops, using plastic wrap to cover the bowl, and transfer to the fridge for ½ hour.

9. Remove the chops from the brine, rinse with cold water, and pat dry using kitchen paper towels.

10. Transfer, 50 percent of the BBQ sauce to a shallow baking dish, while reserving the remaining sauce. Coat both sides of the chops in the sauce.

11. On a moderate heat, and in a grill pan, grill the pork chops until cooked through, 5-6 minutes each side; baste the chops on both sides with the sauce during the grilling process.

12. Remove the chops from the grill and allow to stand for several minutes.

13. Serve with any remaining sauce.

Hawaii - Steamed Mahi-Mahi Laulau

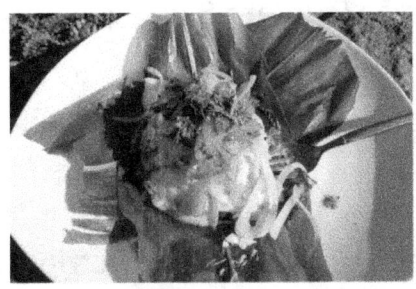

Steaming fish in banana leaves and grilling over a fire is a time old Hawaiian way of cooking. However, with a handful of ingredients and vegetables, you too can create one of the Island's favorite recipes.

Portions: 4

Prep Time: 20mins
Total Time: 30mins

Ingredients:

- 1 pack (1 pound) frozen, thawed banana leaves
- Warm water
- 1½ pounds Mahi-mahi fillets (rinsed, pat dry)
- 2 tsp coarse sea salt
- 1 carrot (scrubbed, peeled)
- 1 red bell pepper (stem, inside ribs trimmed)

- 8 green onions (white/pale green parts only)
- 1 tbsp. butter
- 1 (4") piece fresh ginger (peeled, minced)
- 2 medium limes (cut into 8 wedges)
- 1½ tbsp. sea salt

Directions:

1. Soak the banana leaves in warm tap water until softened and tear 12, narrow, long strips from 2 leaves and boil for 40 seconds; drain. Cut the remaining banana leaves with the grain into 2 dozen strips; each approximately 12x3".

2. Cut the Mahi-mahi into 12 (2x2" each) pieces and sprinkle each side with sea salt. Chill in the refrigerator for 30 minutes.

3. In the meantime, cut the carrot along with the red pepper and onions into lengths of 2", and into very fine slivers.

4. In a pan, over moderate heat, melt the butter. Add the veggies and sauté for 3-4 minutes, or until just soft but not brown. Remove the pan from the heat.

5. Place 2 strips of leaves, shiny sides facing down, on top of one another in the shape of a cross.

6. Place 1 piece of Mahi-mahi in the center of each cross, then top with a heaped tablespoon of the veggie mixture.

7. Starting with the lower strip, fold the banana leaves over the filling, alternating strips and using each of the new strips to fold the loose end of the previous strip completely over the filling. The final strip needs to be tucked beneath the packed, before being tied and closed with boiled leaf strips. Repeat the process with the remaining strips, Mahi-mahi, and vegetables.

8. Over a large pan with a steamer basket, add cold water to approximately ½" below the top of the basket. Over high heat, bring to a swift boil.

9. Place the Mahi-mahi parcels in a single layer in the basket and cover the pan with a tight-fitting lid.

10. Steam the fish for 6-10 minutes, or until the Mahi-mahi is just opaque in its center, taking care not to overcook.

11. Tip the fish parcels to drain away any water.

12. Serve hot with wedges of lime and seasoned with sea salt.

Idaho - French Potato Casserole

Boil them, mash them, fry them, bake them; potatoes have to be one of the most versatile vegetables on the planet!

It's no wonder that every American eats on average 140 pounds each year. What great news this is for Idahoans whose high-quality potatoes have put the state firmly on the potato producing world map.

It is only fitting that this potato casserole flies the flag for this fertile state.

Portions: 4

Prep Time: 10mins

Total Time: 9hours 5mins

Ingredients:

- 1 tbsp. oil (to grease)
- 12 cups (4 pounds) Idaho potatoes (chopped into ¼" cubes)
- 1 cup of Monterey Jack cheese (grated)
- 3 cups of Canadian bacon (cooked, diced)
- 3 jalapeño peppers (seeded and finely chopped)
- ¾ cup scallions (sliced)
- 12 medium eggs (beaten)
- ¾ cup milk
- ¾ tsp pepper

Directions:

1. Lightly grease a 13x9" casserole dish with oil.

2. Evenly place the potatoes in the casserole dish and bake for 10 minutes in an oven set at 350 degrees F

3. Stir and sprinkle with shredded Monterey Jack cheese, cooked bacon, jalapeno pepper and sliced scallions.

4. In a small bowl, combine the eggs along with the milk and jalapeno pepper, stirring to incorporate.

5. Pour the egg mixture over the cubed potatoes.

6. Cover the dish with a lid and place in the refrigerator overnight.

7. Remove the lid and bake at 350 degrees F for 35-45 minutes; until the cubes of potatoes are fork tender.

8. Remove from the oven and allow to stand for several minutes before serving.

Conclusion

This American cookbook has shown you how to use different ingredients to affect sweet or spicy tastes in some American dishes you have heard of, and some you may not be familiar with.

America is a melting pot, resulting from the immigrants who came here from all over the world. Because of this, American cuisine includes many types of ingredients and techniques.

So, what can you do now? After you've breezed through this book, you can...

• Prepare a cookout for the 4th of July (Independence Day) or Memorial Day, complete with grilled foods that will tempt your friends.
• Try your hand at Southern cooking – it's not all fried, and there are some interesting dishes you may want to create for your family.
• Get right to the heart of American cooking with meat and potatoes. Seriously– there are so many dishes that include meat and potatoes, you'll be sure to find one or more you enjoy.
• Offer your family the best comfort food American cuisine has to offer. From pot pies to chili and soup, there's nothing better than warming up with a dish like

this on a cold day.
• Seafood abounds on the East, Gulf and West coasts of America. You'll find many types of dishes that include succulent seafood.

Have fun experimenting! Enjoy the results!

Part 2

Chapter 1: Autumn Season Breakfast Recipes

1) Pumpkin Oatmeal

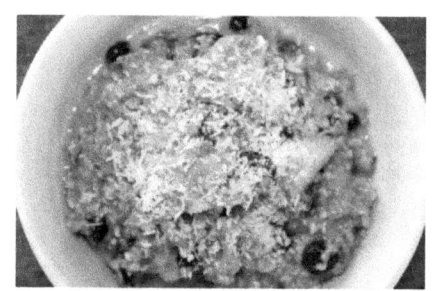

Prep time: 10 minutes
Cook time: 5 minutes
Servings: 2

Ingredients:

- 2 cups quick-cooking oats
- ½ teaspoon cinnamon
- 1/3 teaspoon pumpkin pie spice
- ½ cup canned pumpkin
- 4 cups of milk
- brown sugar to taste
- raisins for topping

- walnuts for topping

Directions:
1. In a saucepan, over medium-high heat add milk and bring to a boil.
2. Add your oats into the pan along with milk and cook for about 5 minutes or until the mixture thickens.
3. Stir in your cinnamon, pumpkin puree and pumpkin spice.
4. Serve with a dash of brown sugar, walnuts and raisins on top and enjoy!

2) Cinnamon Scones

Prep time: 5 minutes
Cook time: 20 minutes
Servings: 12

Ingredients:

- 4 cups flour
- 1 cup sour cream
- 1 teaspoon baking soda
- 1 cup of sugar
- 1 cup butter
- 1 egg
- 4 teaspoon cinnamon
- 1 teaspoon salt
- ¼ teaspoon cream of tartar
- 2 teaspoons baking powder

Directions:

1. Your first step is to preheat your oven to 350° Fahrenheit, and grease cookie sheets.

2. In a small mixing bowl, combine your baking soda and sour cream.

3. Combine your dry ingredients in another bowl. Crumble in the butter until crumbly.

4. Add egg to sour cream mixture, and add cinnamon. Gently stir into flour mixture to batter is moist. Knead your dough briefly.

5. Divide your dough into two, place on two cookie sheets, and pat to ¾ inch thick scones. Six scones on each cookie sheet.

6. Slice into wedge pieces, move scones, so they are not touching, then dust with cinnamon and sugar. Bake for 20 minutes.

3) Sweet Potato Omelet

Prep Time: 15 minutes
Cook time: 5 minutes
Servings: 2

Ingredients:

- 4 eggs beaten
- 2 tablespoons milk
- 6-ounces feta cheese, crumbled
- 4 tablespoons olive oil
- salt and pepper to taste
- 1 ½ lb. Sweet potato, boiled and sliced thinly

Directions:

1. Heat the oil in a skillet over medium-high heat.

2. Add sweet potatoes to the pan and cook for 3 minutes.

3. Mix eggs and two tablespoons of milk in a small mixing bowl. Pour mixture into the pan along with potatoes. Add the cheese into the pan. Cook for another couple of minutes, then sprinkle top with salt and pepper to taste.

4. Serve and enjoy!

4) Oven-Baked Egg Wraps

Prep time: 8 minutes
Cook time: 33 minutes
Servings: 10

Ingredients:

- 12 eggs
- 1 lb. Italian sausage links, with the casing, removed
- 1 onion, diced finely
- 1 sweet red pepper, diced
- 10 (8-inch) flour tortillas
- 1 teaspoon chili powder
- 1 ¼ cup of salsa

Directions:

1. Begin by spraying a 13×9 casserole dish with cooking spray and set aside.

2. Add the sausage to a small pan and cook and crumble until browned.

3. Drain the sausage and layer into the casserole dish.

4. Spread the diced onion and red pepper over top of sausage.

5. Beat the eggs in a mixing bowl, then add to the casserole dish. Bake for 30 minutes or until set.

6. Use a fork to help you to break up the eggs, then allow it to cool.

7. Place tortilla out flat and then top with some salsa. Add about ½ cup of eggs on top of salsa.

8. Fold your tortilla over mixture tucking in the sides. Place in a freezer bag and freeze.

9. To reheat your tortilla, remove from the freezer bag and place onto a microwave-safe plate. Cook in your microwave for about 3 minutes or until heated through.

10. Serve and enjoy!

5) Applesauce Oatmeal Pancakes

Prep time: 10 minutes
Cook time: 5 minutes
Servings: 24 pancakes

Ingredients:

- 1 ½ cups flour
- 1 ½ cups milk
- 1 ½ cups oats
- ½ teaspoon salt
- 2 teaspoon baking powder
- 6 egg whites
- 1 ½ cup applesauce, unsweetened
- 3 tablespoons canola oil
- ¾ cup brown sugar

Directions:

1. Preheat your skillet over medium-high heat. Put all of your ingredients into a mixing bowl and mix with a hand mixer until smooth.

2. Drop spoonfuls of batter onto your hot griddle. Cook for a few minutes per side or until browned on both sides.

3. Add pancakes to cookie sheet then flash freeze them for several hours. Remove from sheet and place pancakes into Ziploc baggie.

4. When you are ready to eat pancakes, reheat in the microwave.

5. Serve and enjoy!

Chapter 2: Autumn Season Lunch Recipes

1) Squash & Cilantro Fall Soup

Prep time: 10 minutes
Cook time: 30 minutes
Servings: 2

Ingredients:

- 2 cups hot water
- 2 cubes of chicken bouillon, crumbled
- 2 squashes, peeled and sliced into 1/2-inch pieces
- 1 yellow onion, minced
- 1 tablespoon butter, unsalted
- ¼ teaspoon mashed red pepper flakes
- 2 tablespoons cilantro, fresh, chopped
- 1 tablespoon cilantro, fresh, chopped for garnish
- salt and pepper to taste

Directions:

1. In a pan, cook the red pepper, onion, garlic in hot butter for a few minutes.

2. Add the 2 tablespoons cilantro, squash, salt and pepper and cook for another 5 minutes.

3. Stir in the chicken bouillon (which has been dissolved in hot water). Continue to cook for 20 minutes on low.

4. Carefully use your blender to blend until smooth.

5. Add to serving bowls, and top with chopped cilantro for garnish.

6. Serve and enjoy!

2) New England Style Chowder

Prep time: 8 minutes
Cook time: 35 minutes
Servings: 2

Ingredients:

- 4 potatoes, peeled and cubed
- 4 slices of bacon
- ½ cup onion, chopped
- 2 (6-ounce) cans minced clams
- 2 tablespoons parsley, fresh chopped
- salt and pepper to taste
- ½ cup heavy cream

- 1 cup half-and-half
- 1 cup bottled clam juice
- 1 tablespoon all-purpose flour

Directions:

1. Cook bacon over medium-high heat for about 10 minutes. Crumble then set it aside.

2. Cook the potatoes and onions in the pan for about 5 minutes. Add in flour to the pan and stir to combine well.

3. Next, add the clam juice and bring to a boil. Set your stove to low and cook for an additional 15 minutes.

4. Stir in the minced clams, half-and-half, heavy cream, salt and pepper, and cook for another 5 minutes.

5. Add to serving bowls, and top with some chopped parsley and crumbled bacon for garnish.

6. Serve and enjoy!

3) Cream Of Hash Browns Fall Casserole

Prep time: 10 minutes
Cook time: 45 minutes
Servings: 2

Ingredients:

- 1 ½ cup sour cream
- 2 (10-75-ounce) can condensed cream of chicken soup
- 1 (2 lb.) package frozen shredded hash brown potatoes, thawed
- 2 tablespoons dried minced onion flakes
- 2 tablespoons butter, softened
- 4-ounces extra-sharp Cheddar cheese, shredded
- ½ cup mashed cornflakes cereal
- ground black pepper to taste

Directions:

1. Set your oven to 350° Fahrenheit.

2. Combine sour cream, soup, half of your cheese, dried onion, hash browns, pepper and butter into mixing bowl and stir to combine. Pour mixture into baking dish.

3. Bake mixture in your preheated oven for 45 minutes.

4. Serve and enjoy!

4) Pumpkin Soup

Prep time: 5 minutes
Cook time: 50 minutes
Servings: 2

Ingredients:

- ¼ cup sour cream
- 2 sugar pumpkins, halved and seeded
- 3 cups chicken broth
- 1 ½ teaspoon salt
- ¼ teaspoon ground nutmeg
- ½ teaspoon ground sage, crushed
- ¾ cup heavy whipping cream

Directions:

1. Set your oven to 400° Fahrenheit. Grease a baking sheet.

2. Place cut pumpkin slices on the baking sheet with the cut side facing down.

3. Roast the pumpkin pieces for 45 minutes.

4. Remove the pumpkin pieces from the oven and allow to cool.

5. After the pumpkin pieces are cooled, scrape out the flesh of the pumpkin.

6. Collect pumpkin flesh into the food processor, add in broth and pulse until smooth.

7. Bring in a pot to a simmer, then stir in sage, whipping cream, nutmeg, and salt.

8. Transfer the soup to serving bowls.

9. Top your soup with a dollop of sour cream.

10. Serve hot and enjoy!

5) Pumpkin Autumn Chili

Prep time: 10 minutes
Cook time: 30 minutes
Servings: 2

Ingredients:

- 1 lb. Ground turkey
- 1 tablespoon olive oil
- 1 cup onion, chopped
- ½ cup sour cream
- ½ cup cheddar cheese, shredded
- ½ teaspoon freshly ground black pepper
- 1 ½ tablespoon red chilli powder
- 1 (141/2-ounces) can of tomatoes, diced
- 2 cups pumpkin puree

- 1 garlic clove, minced
- ½ cup yellow bell pepper, seeded and chopped
- ½ cup green bell pepper, seeded and chopped
- sea salt to taste

Directions:

1. First, start by heating your olive oil in a large pan over medium-high heat.

2. Add your bell peppers, onion, and garlic to the pan and sauté for 5 minutes.

3. Place your ground turkey into the pan, and cook for 5 minutes or until browned.

4. Drain any excess fat from the pan.

5. Add the pumpkin puree, tomatoes and seasoning to the pan and stir to combine.

6. Bring pumpkin chili to a gentle boil. Reduce the heat to low.

7. Simmer, pumpkin chili covered for 20 minutes.

8. Transfer pumpkin chili to serving bowls, and top with sour cream and shredded cheese.

9. Serve hot and enjoy!

Chapter 3: Autumn Dinner Recipes

1) Autumn Baked Whole Chicken

Prep time: 5 minutes
Cook time: 107 minutes
Servings: 4

Ingredients:

- 1 (4 lb.) whole chicken
- 2 carrots, sliced into chunks
- 8 slices bacon
- 2 cups chicken broth
- 1 teaspoon thyme, dried
- 2 tablespoons butter
- paprika to taste

- salt and pepper to taste

Directions:

1. Set your oven to 450° Fahrenheit before you do anything else.

2. Coat your chicken with butter, paprika, thyme, pepper and salt.

3. Fill your chicken with the slices of carrots and then string the legs together.

4. Carefully lay out the bacon strips on the top of the chicken, using toothpicks to hold them in place.

5. Place your chicken into a roasting pan, then pour the broth around the chicken, but not on top of it.

6. Cook for 17 minutes with the oven set at 350° Fahrenheit and cook for an additional 80 minutes. Baste the chicken throughout the cooking time.

7. Remove the bacon from the chicken. Baste the top of the chicken, then cook for another 15 minutes or until the skin is brown and crispy.

8. Serve and enjoy!

2) Apple & Cheddar Autumn Stuffed Chicken Breast

Prep time: 9 minutes
Cook time: 30 minutes
Servings: 2

Ingredients:

- 2 chicken breasts, boneless and skinless
- 2 tablespoons Cheddar cheese, shredded
- ½ cup apple, chopped
- 1 tablespoon butter
- ¼ cup dry white wine
- 1 tablespoon parsley, fresh and chopped for garnish
- 1 ½ teaspoon cornstarch

- 1 tablespoon water
- 1 tablespoon Italian-style dried bread crumbs

Directions:

1. In a mixing bowl, mix your breadcrumbs, apple and cheese.

2. Place your chicken breasts between 2 sheets of wax paper and using a meat mallet flatten chicken breasts to 1/4-inch thickness.

3. Add the mixture into the centre of chicken breasts spread evenly.

4. Roll each chicken breast around in the filling and secure with toothpicks.

5. Melt your butter in a large pan, over medium heat and cook the chicken breasts until browned completely.

6. Add ¼ cup water and wine, simmer covered for about 20 minutes.

7. Transfer the chicken breasts to a plate.

8. In a bowl, mix cornstarch and remaining water together. Add to pan with juices and cook until the gravy becomes thick.

9. Pour the gravy over the chicken breasts, then garnish with fresh chopped parsley.

10. Serve and enjoy!

3) Turkey Pot Pie

Prep time: 8 minutes
Cook time: 50 minutes
Servings: 4

Ingredients:

- 1 lb. Ground turkey
- 1 tablespoon olive oil
- 1 onion, diced
- 6 tablespoons butter, cut into pieces
- 1 cup milk
- 1 ½ lb. Russet potatoes, peeled and cut into 1 ½-inch piece
- cooking spray
- 1 cup of water

- 1 (16-ounce) package frozen peas and carrots, thawed
- 2 cups shredded cheese, your choice
- salt and pepper to taste

Directions:

1. Start by spraying your casserole dish with cooking spray and set your oven to 350° Fahrenheit.

2. Boil your Russet potatoes, then remove the liquids and mash them.

3. Add milk, butter, salt and pepper with your potatoes and mash to combine.

4. In a small pan, stir fry your onions and turkey in 1 tablespoon oil until the turkey is cooked.

5. Add to your turkey the water, gravy, pepper and salt.

6. Simmer your gravy until it thickens.

7. Add your turkey to the casserole dish, then add a layer of carrots and peas, and finally cover with a layer of mashed potatoes.

8. Sprinkle top of mashed potatoes with your choice of shredded cheese.

9. Cook your turkey casserole dish for 30 minutes. After casserole is cooked, let it sit for 10 minutes before serving.

10. Serve hot and enjoy!

4) Country Time Chili

Prep time: 15 minutes
Cook time: 25 minutes
Servings: 6

Ingredients:

- 1 lb. Ground beef
- 1 cup penne macaroni
- 1 yellow onion, diced
- 1/8 cup brown sugar
- 2 (14.5-ounce) cans tomatoes, diced
- 2 (10.75-ounce) cans condensed tomato soup
- 1 (15-ounce) can kidney beans, drained, rinsed
- ½ large green pepper, diced
- 1 cup celery, diced
- salt and pepper to taste

Directions:

1. Boil your elbow macaroni in water for 9 minutes then remove the liquid.

2. Boil your green pepper and celery in water for 5 minutes, then remove the liquid.

3. Stir fry your ground beef until it is fully browned, combine with onions and cook onions until they become see-through.

4. Add the celery mix with meat and also add in kidney beans, brown sugar, and tomato soup.

5. Simmer for 10 minutes and stir to combine, then turn off the heat and add the pasta along with some salt and pepper.

6. Serve hot and enjoy!

5) Autumn 3 Bean Vegetarian Chili

Prep time: 10 minutes
Cook time: 2 hours
Servings: 8

Ingredients:

- 1 (15-ounce) can of garbanzo beans, rinsed and drained
- 1 (14.5-ounce) can diced tomatoes puree
- 1 (16-ounce) can vegetarian baked beans
- 1 (15-ounce) can of kidney beans, rinsed and drained
- 1 (19-ounce) can black bean soup
- 1 onion, diced
- 1 green bell pepper, diced

- 2 cloves garlic, diced
- 2 stalks celery, diced
- 1 tablespoon dried parsley
- 1 tablespoon chili powder
- 1 tablespoon dried oregano
- 1 tablespoon dried basil
- 1 (15-ounce) can of whole kernel corn, drained

Directions:

1. Add the ingredients to your Crockpot. Stir to combine ingredients and mix well.

2. Set your Crockpot to high and cook for 3 hours.

3. Allow the chili to sit for 20 minutes before serving.

4. Try serving with a nice dollop of sour cream on top.

5. Serve hot and enjoy!

6) Shrimp Tempura

Prep time: 45 minutes
Cook time: 15 minutes
Servings: 8

Ingredients:

- ½ lb. Fresh shrimp, peeled and deveined
- ½ cup of rice wine
- ¼ teaspoon of sea salt
- 2 quarts oil for deep frying
- ½ teaspoon baking powder
- 1 teaspoon shortening
- ¼ teaspoon white sugar
- ¼ teaspoon of sea salt
- ¼ cup cornstarch
- 1/3 cup ice water
- ¼ cup all-purpose flour

Directions:

1. Mix rice wine and ¼ teaspoon of sea salt in a bowl.

2. Coat your shrimp with the rice wine mixture, then refrigerate for 20 minutes.

3. Combine the white sugar, all-purpose flour, ice water, cornstarch, salt, egg yolk, shortening and baking powder in a mixing bowl.

4. Coat your shrimp with the flour mixture, then deep fry shrimp in hot oil for about 2 minutes or until shrimp are a golden brown on all sides.

5. Drain shrimp onto a paper towel.

6. Serve and enjoy!

7) Autumn Meat Loaf & Oats

Prep time: 10 minutes
Cook time: 1 hour
Servings: 1 (8-inch) square pan

Ingredients:

- 1 lb. Ground beef
- 2 eggs, beaten
- 1 can French onion soup
- 1 ½ cups rolled oats

Directions:

1. Set your oven to 375° Fahrenheit.

2. In a mixing bowl, combine your beaten eggs, oats, beef, and onion soup.

3. Place ingredients into your loaf pan.

4. Bake meatloaf for 1 hour and 20 minutes. Make sure the meatloaf has an internal temperature of 160 degrees before removing it from your oven.

5. Serve hot and enjoy!

8) Fall Spinach Salad

Prep time: 10 minutes
Cook time: 10 minutes
Servings: 8

Ingredients:

- 1 lb. Fresh spinach, torn
- 1 cup dried cranberries
- ¾ cup almonds, blanched and slivered
- 1 tablespoon butter

For Dressing:
- ¼ cup cider vinegar
- ½ cup of vegetable oil
- ½ cup white sugar
- ¼ cup white wine vinegar
- 2 tablespoons sesame seeds, toasted

- 2 teaspoons onion, minced
- ¼ teaspoon paprika
- 1 tablespoon poppy seeds

Directions:

1. In a small pan, melt the butter over medium heat.

2. Add the almonds to the pan and cook for about 10 minutes.

3. Remove almonds from heat and allow them to cool.

4. In a large bowl, mix spinach, almonds, and cranberries.

5. In another bowl, add all of the dressing ingredients and beat till well combined.

6. Pour the dressing over salad and toss to coat.

7. Serve immediately and enjoy!

9) Fall Pumpkin & Chicken

Prep time: 15 minutes
Cook time: 30 minutes
Servings: 4

Ingredients:

- 2 chicken breasts, boneless and skinless, sliced into bite-size pieces
- 1 ½ cup chicken broth
- ½ cup of canned coconut milk
- 1 (2 lb.) sugar pumpkin, peeled, seeded and cubed
- pinch of ground turmeric
- 1 teaspoon red pepper flakes, crushed
- 1 tablespoon ground cumin
- 2 garlic cloves, minced
- 1 (1-inch) piece fresh ginger, finely chopped
- 1 tablespoon butter

- 1 tablespoon olive oil
- 1 teaspoon poultry seasoning
- sea salt to taste

Directions:

1. Coat your chicken with the poultry seasoning, then set aside for 5 minutes.

2. In a skillet, heat your oil over medium heat.

3. Place your chicken into the pan and cook for 5 minutes. Put the chicken in a bowl and set aside.

4. In the same skillet, melt your butter over medium heat.

5. Add in the onion and sauté for about 4 minutes.

6. Add the spices, garlic and ginger and sauté for an additional minute or so.

7. Stir in the pumpkin, coconut milk, broth, and cook chicken. Bring to a boil.

8. Keep covered for about 20 minutes or until desired thickness.

9. Season with sea salt and remove from heat.

10. Serve hot and enjoy!

10) Autumn Pumpkin Curry

Prep time: 20 minutes
Cook time: 1 hour and 55 minutes
Servings: 6

Ingredients:

- 1 cup red lentils
- 1 cup brown lentils
- 8 cups of water
- ½ teaspoon ground turmeric
- 1 tablespoon canola oil
- ½ teaspoon freshly ground black pepper
- ½ teaspoon of sea salt
- 2 teaspoons ground cumin
- 1 ½ tablespoon ground curry powder
- ¼ teaspoon ground cloves

- 2 carrots, peeled and chopped
- 2 potatoes, scrubbed and chopped
- 2 cups pumpkin, peeled, seeded, and cubed into 1-inch size
- 2 tomatoes, seeded and chopped
- 3 garlic cloves, minced
- 1 large onion, chopped
- 2 cups fresh spinach, packed and torn
- 1 granny smith apple, cored and chopped

Directions:

1. In a pan, add water, both lentils and turmeric, over medium-low heat.

2. Cover pan and cook for 45 minutes.

3. Drain, however, reserve 2 ½ cups of cooking liquid.

4. In a large pan, heat oil over medium heat.

5. Add your onion to the pan and sauté for 5 minutes.

6. Add tomatoes and garlic to the pan and cook for 5 minutes while stirring to combine.

7. Stir in the cooked lentils, reserved liquid, potatoes, carrots, spices, and curry powder.

8. Bring to a gentle boil, then reduce heat to medium-low. Cook, covered for about 45 minutes.

9. Stir in the spinach and apple and simmer for about 15 minutes.

10. Season with salt and pepper, then serve hot and enjoy!

11) Autumn Lo-Mein

Prep time: 45 minutes
Cook time: 30 minutes
Servings: 4

Ingredients:

- ½ lb. Fresh Shiitake mushrooms, stemmed and sliced
- 6 green onions, sliced into 1/2-inch pieces
- 1 tablespoon garlic, diced
- 2 tablespoons fresh ginger root, diced
- 1 (12-ounce) package uncooked linguine pasta
- ½ teaspoon ground black pepper
- 2 tablespoons cornstarch
- 1 cup of water

- 1 tablespoon sesame oil
- 1 ¼ cup chicken broth
- 3 tablespoons of rice wine vinegar
- ½ cup soy sauce, divided
- 5 teaspoons white sugar, divided
- 4 chicken breast halves-sliced into thin strips, skinless and boneless

Directions:

1. Begin with boiling your pasta in salted water for about 10 minutes or until al dente. Drain the liquid and set aside.

2. In a bowl mix, 1.5 teaspoons sugar, 1.4 cup soy sauce, and 1.5 tablespoons vinegar. Add in your chicken strips and cover the bowl with some plastic. Place in the fridge for 2 hours.

3. In another bowl, mix broth, black pepper, sesame oil, water and remaining sugar.

4. In a third mixing bowl, mix the cornstarch with some of the sesame mix.

5. Combine the second and third bowl mixtures.

6. Now begin to stir fry your chicken for about six minutes in veggie oil in a wok. Set aside. Then add some more oil to stir fry your mushrooms, onions, ginger, and garlic for 1 minute.

7. Add the cornstarch mixture and cook for about 5 minutes or until it becomes thick.

8. Add the noodles to the mix and toss to evenly coat noodles with sauce.

9. Serve and enjoy!

12) Fall Shiitake & Pasta

Prep time: 8 minutes
Cook time: 15 minutes
Servings: 4

Ingredients:

- 6-ounces fresh Shiitake mushrooms, sliced
- 6-ounces your favorite pasta
- 2 tablespoons grated Parmesan cheese
- ½ white onion, diced
- ¼ cup white wine
- ½ cup heavy whipping cream
- ¼ cup chicken broth
- 1 clove garlic, diced
- 1 tablespoon olive oil
- sea salt to taste

- ground black pepper to taste
- 2 tablespoons fresh parsley, diced

Directions:

1. Boil your angel hair pasta in salt water for about 10 minutes. Remove the liquid and set the pasta aside.

2. Stir fry your garlic and onions until they become aromatic, then add the mushrooms, wine and broth to pan.

3. Cook until half of the liquid has been evaporated. Add salt and pepper to taste.

4. Add the sauce to pasta and stir to coat evenly.

5. Garnish with Parmesan and parsley.

6. Serve and enjoy!

13) Autumn Beef With Mushroom Sauce

Prep time: 30 minutes
Cook time: 20 minutes
Servings: 4

Ingredients:

- 4 (8-ounce) filet mignon steaks
- 2 tablespoons Mirin (Japanese sweet wine)
- 3 tablespoons sake
- 1 tablespoon garlic chives, finely diced
- ½ cup unsalted butter
- ½ teaspoon of sea salt
- ½ cup fresh Shiitake mushrooms, thinly sliced
- 1 tablespoon garlic, finely diced

- 2 tablespoons fresh ginger, finely diced
- 3 tablespoons unsalted butter
- 2 tablespoons olive oil
- sea salt and black pepper to taste

Directions:

1. Set your oven to 400° Fahrenheit.

2. Sear your steaks in olive oil for 4 minutes per side, after seasoning with salt and pepper.

3. Bake everything in your oven for about 12 minutes. Then place the steaks to the side.

4. Get a mixing bowl and combine the sake and mirin.

5. Stir fry the garlic and ginger, along with 3 tablespoons of butter for 3 minutes. Add in mushrooms and a teaspoon of salt.

6. Cook the mushrooms for about 5 minutes, then add in the mirin mix and let it continue to cook until half of the liquid has evaporated.

7. Add in half a cup of butter. Melt your butter down over low heat and let it brown for about 9 minutes.

8. Add in the chives along with salt and pepper to taste.

9. Top the steaks with brown mushroom sauce.

10. Serve and enjoy!

Chapter 4: Autumn Dessert Recipes

1) Autumn Apple Crisp

Prep time: 20 minutes
Cook time: 40 minutes
Servings: 6

Ingredients:

- 4 cups apples, peeled, cored, sliced
- ½ cup cold butter
- ¾ cup all-purpose flour
- 1 cup white sugar
- 1 teaspoon ground cinnamon

Directions:

1. Set your oven to 350° Fahrenheit and lightly grease an 8×8-inch casserole dish.

2. Place your apples at the bottom of the prepared casserole dish.

3. Drizzle with evenly with water and cinnamon.

4. In a mixing bowl, mix the sugar and flour.

5. Cut the butter using a pastry cutter, and mix till the crumbly mix is formed.

6. Place crumble mixture over top of apple slices. Cook in the oven for about 40 minutes.

7. Serve and enjoy!

2) Favorite Autumn Apple Dessert

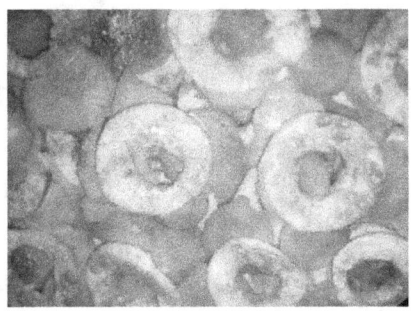

Prep time: 10 minutes
Cook time: 20 minutes
Servings: 8

Ingredients:

- 2 large Honey-crisp apples, diced
- 2 large sweet potatoes, peeled and diced
- 2/3 cup water
- 2 teaspoons ground cinnamon
- 2 tablespoons butter, diced
- ½ teaspoon ground nutmeg

Directions:

1. Set your oven to 425° Fahrenheit.

2. Arrange the slices of apples and sweet potatoes in the bottom of a microwave-safe loaf pan. Sprinkle them with some cinnamon and nutmeg.

3. Add enough water to the pan to cover about 1/2-inch of the base and cook in the microwave for 8 minutes.

4. Drain well.

5. Place the butter over the apple mixture and then finish cooking in the oven for about 10 minutes.

6. Serve and Enjoy!

3) Fall Pumpkin Pie

Prep time: 15 minutes
Cook time: 40 minutes
Servings: 8

Ingredients:

- 2 teaspoons ground cinnamon
- 1 cup packed brown sugar
- 2 tablespoons molasses
- 1 cup evaporated milk
- 1 (15-ounce) can of pumpkin puree
- ½ teaspoon salt
- 1 teaspoon ground ginger
- 3 eggs, beaten
- 1 (9-inch) single pie crust

Directions:

1. Set your oven to 425° Fahrenheit. Grease pie pan, add pie crust to the pan.

2. In mixing bowl, combine your brown sugar and spices.

3. Add pumpkin puree, eggs, milk, and molasses, mix until well combined.

4. Transfer pumpkin mixture to your pie crust. Bake for 40 minutes.

5. Serve and enjoy!

4) Fall Rhubarb Dumplings

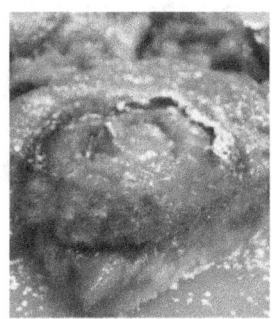

Prep time: 15 minutes
Cook time: 40 minutes
Servings: 10

Ingredients:

- 2 cups fresh rhubarb, chopped
- 1 (12-ounce) can of refrigerated buttermilk biscuit dough
- 1 cup white sugar
- ¼ teaspoon ground cinnamon
- 1 ¼ teaspoon vanilla extract
- ½ cup butter, melted
- 1 cup of water

Directions:

1. Set your oven to 350° Fahrenheit.

2. Make 3-inch circles from biscuit dough and then fold around the rhubarb placed at its center.

3. Place the dumplings onto a baking dish, then pour a mixture of sugar, butter, water, and vanilla over it then sprinkle with cinnamon.

4. Bake for 40 minutes in your preheated oven or until the biscuits are golden brown.

5. Serve and enjoy!

5) Fall Time Muffins

Prep time: 15 minutes
Cook time: 45 minutes
Servings: 18

Ingredients:

- 2 ½ cups all-purpose flour
- 4 teaspoons butter
- 2 cups white sugar
- 2 eggs, lightly beaten
- 1 tablespoon pumpkin pie spice
- ½ teaspoon salt
- 1 teaspoon baking soda
- 1 can of pumpkin puree
- ½ cup vegetable oil
- 2 cups apples, peeled, cored and chopped
    ½ teaspoon ground cinnamon

Directions:

1. First, set your oven to 350° Fahrenheit, and grease 18 cup muffin tray.

2. In a large mixing bowl, sift together 2 ½ cups flour, 2 cups of sugar, baking soda, pumpkin pie spice, and salt.

3. In another mixing bowl, add the oil, pumpkin, and eggs, beat until well combined.

4. Add your egg mixture to your flour mixture and mix until well combined.

5. Fold in the apples, then add the mixture to the muffin tray.

6. In another bowl, add the remaining sugar, cinnamon, and flour.

7. Cut the butter using a pastry cutter and mix until crumb forms.

8. Place mixture over each muffin evenly. Cook in the oven for 40 minutes.

9. Serve and enjoy!

Alabama - Pecan Crusted Sweet Potato With Sour Cream

In 1982, the pecan became the official state nut of Alabama. In fact, there are more than 1000 different varieties of pecans, and lots are named after Native American Indian tribes including the Mohawk, Shawnee, Cheyenne, and Sioux.

Did you know, April is National Pecan Month?

Portions: 4-6

Prep Time: 20mins

Total Time: 1hour 10mins

Ingredients:

- 1 large sweet potato (scrubbed, chopped into 1/3" rounds)

- Olive oil
- 3½ ounces whole pecans
- 2 large handfuls Parmesan cheese (freshly grated)
- Small bunch thyme
- 1½ cups sour cream

Ingredients:

1. Preheat the main oven to 400 degrees F.

2. Discard the smaller ends of the sweet potato and arrange the potato slices in a single layer on a parchment paper lined baking tray.

3. Drizzle the slices with olive oil.

4. Finely chop the pecans but leave several chunky pieces.

5. In a bowl, add the chopped nuts to the grated Parmesan and mix to combine.

6. Scatter the nut/cheese mixture evenly over the sliced potato.

7. Sprinkle the fresh thyme on top.

8. Bake in the preheated oven for 45-50 minutes, until the nut crust is just brown and the potato is tender.

Check the potatoes after half an hour and if they are browning a little quickly, cover with aluminum foil.

9. Serve the potatoes hot with sour cream.

Alaska - Caribou Stroganoff

Of course, Alaskans have a great selection of supermarket foods, but they also have access to fresh foods that are indigenous to the state. They not only rely on fishing but also hunting. Bear, moose, and caribou are all animals that provide much-needed protein for anyone living outside the main cities.

Portions: 4-6

Prep Time: 10mins
Total Time: 35mins

Ingredients:

- 1½ pounds caribou steak or boneless stewing meat (cut in 1/2" strips)
- ½ cup flour
- ½ tsp salt

- 1 clove garlic (minced)
- 2 small onions (peeled, chopped)
- ½ pound mushrooms (chopped)
- 3 tbsp. bacon fat
- 1 tbsp. Worcestershire sauce
- 1 beef bouillon cube (dissolved in hot water)
- 1 cup sour cream
- Steamed rice
- Paprika (to garnish)

Directions:

1. Pound the meat to tenderize. *

2. Dredge the beef in flour and salt. Reserve any leftover flour.

3. In a frying pan, sauté the garlic along with the onions and mushrooms in the bacon fat, for 5 minutes.

4. Remove from the pan and add the meat. Cook until brown all over.

5. Remove the meat from the pan and add the remaining flour to the pan drippings.

6. Add the Worcestershire sauce along with the bouillon.

7. Cook the mixture until it begins to thicken and add the sour cream.

8. Heat gently until the gravy just simmers. Return the meat and cooked vegetables to the pan and heat through.

9. Serve over rice and sprinkle with paprika.

*If the meat is very tender or ground you will not need to pound.

Arizona - Navajo Taco

This recipe is based on fry bread, which was created in 1864 using sugar, flour, and lard. The ingredients were given to the Navajo by the US government when the tribe was forced to make the Long Walk; the 300-mile journey to New Mexico.

Portions: 4

Prep Time: 10mins
Total Time: 35mins

Ingredients:

Fry bread:
- 1 (13.8 ounce) can classic pizza dough
- Oil for frying

Taco Filling:

- 1 tbsp. oil
- 1 pound lean ground beef
- 1 (15.5 ounce) can kidney beans (drained, rinsed)
- 1 (10 ounce) diced tomatoes and green chilies
- 1 (4.5 ounce) can chopped green chilies
- 1 tsp each chili powder, cumin, garlic powder, salt

Toppings:

- Shredded cheese
- Chopped tomatoes
- Diced red onion
- Diced green onion
- Chopped cilantro
- Olives
- Avocado/Guacamole
- Salsa
- Sour Cream

Directions:

1. On a lightly floured surface, roll out the dough and cut into 4 evenly sized pieces.

2. Roll each piece into a ball shape and then using the palm of your hand; flatten the ball into a pancake of around ¼" thick. Repeat the process for each piece of dough and put to one side.

3. In the meantime, make the taco filling. Place a frying pan over moderate heat and heat the oil. Add the ground beef and using a wooden spoon, break the meat apart. When it is almost cooked through, crumble the beef using a potato masher.

4. Add the remaining taco ingredients and stir to combine. Cover the pan and reduce the heat to medium to low.

5. Next fry the dough. In a high sided pan, heat 1" of oil on moderate heat for 4-5 minutes. Pinch off one piece of the dough and carefully place it in the hot oil. As soon as it begins to bubble, the oil is ready.

6. Carefully, poke a single hole in each piece of dough; this will ensure that it fries evenly. Place the dough in the oil and using a spatula, gently move it around the pan to prevent it from sticking. Fry for a few minutes on each side. You may need to reduce the heat to avoid it cooking too fast.

7. Transfer the fried dough to a kitchen paper towel-lined serving plate and pat dry; this will remove any excess oil. Place the fry bread on a plate.

8. Drain the liquid from the taco filling.

9. Top the fry bread with the filling and garnish with toppings of choice.

Arkansas - Possum Pie

A four-layer pie known as the secret pie of Arkansas. So-called Possum Pie because the dessert pretends to be something it's not, as the whipped cream exterior hides the chocolatey filling inside.

Portions: 8

Prep Time: 15mins

Total Time: 4hours 15mins

Ingredients:

- 1 cup flour
- 1 cup + 1 tbsp. pecans (finely chopped)
- 1 stick butter (melted)
- 4 ounces full-fat cream cheese (softened)
- ½ cup confectioners' sugar

- 1 (8 ounce) container frozen whip topping (thawed, divided)
- 1 (4-serving size) package instant chocolate fudge pudding and pie filling
- 1½ cups whole milk

Directions:

1. Preheat the main oven to 350 degrees F.

2. In a mixing bowl, combine the flour along with 1 cup of pecans, and the stick of butter and using a fork mix until incorporated.

3. Press the mixture into a deep (9") pie dish plate, to form a crust.

4. Transfer to the oven for 15-20 minutes, until the crust begins to brown. Put to one side to cool.

5. In a medium-sized mixing bowl, beat the cream cheese together with the sugar until silky. Add 1 cup of whip topping and mix until incorporated.

6. Evenly spread the mixture over the pie crust.

7. In a third mixing bowl, whisk the fudge pudding and whole milk until it begins to thicken. Spread the mixture evenly on top of the cream cheese.

8. Spoon the remaining whip cream on the top of the pie and scatter with remaining chopped pecans.

9. Transfer to the fridge to chill for 3-4 hours before serving.

California - Grilled Artichokes With Californian Avocado

Did you know that 99.99% of commercially grown artichokes come from the state of California and that the official fruit of California is the avocado?

This recipe combines two of the Golden State's most important produce in one delicious, vegan dish.

Portions: 2-4

Prep Time: 15mins

Total Time: 1hour 15mins

Ingredients:

- 2 large Californian artichokes (trimmed)

- 2 cups cold water
- 2 cups vegan white wine
- 1 head garlic (divided)
- Sea salt and black pepper
- 1 tsp virgin olive oil
- 2 ripe, fresh Californian avocados (peeled, pitted)
- Zest and juice of 1 lemon
- 4 tbsp. parsley (chopped)

Directions:

1. Preheat the main oven to 400 degrees F.

2. Cut the artichokes in half, and using a spoon, clean out the thistle above the hearts and discard.

3. Arrange the artichokes in a shallow ovenproof pan filled with water and wine.

4. Take 2 cloves of garlic and smash. Set to one side.

5. Roughly chop and smash the remaining garlic and put it in the pan along with the artichokes.

6. Transfer the pan to the oven for 45-60 minutes, or until the artichokes are tender and beginning to fall apart. Remove them from the pan and drain.

7. Season each artichoke half with salt and pepper and drizzle with virgin olive oil.

8. Preheat the grill until it is extremely hot. Arrange the artichokes on the grill until grill marks become visible. Remove from the pan and set to one side.

9. Smash the avocado and transfer to a separate bowl along with the reserved garlic, lemon zest and juice, and parsley. Mix to combine. Season with sea salt and adjust if necessary.

10. Spoon the avocado mixture into the halves of artichokes and serve.

Colorado - Classic Denver Omelet

This classic breakfast dish is also known as the Denver sandwich or Western omelet. It is believed that it was initially created by Chinese cooks who, when working on the railroad, put egg foo yung between bread.

It's made from eggs, ham, pepper, and onion. This particular recipe has the filling cooked directly into the egg instead of the more traditional method.

Portions: 1

Prep Time: 10mins
Total Time: 30mins

Ingredients:

- 2 tsp butter
- 2 tbsp. cooked ham (chopped)

- 1 tbsp. bell pepper (chopped)
- 1 tbsp. onion (chopped)
- 2 medium eggs (beaten)

Directions:

1. In an 8" omelet pan over moderate to high heat, heat the butter until it begins to just brown. Swirl the melted butter; tilt the omelet pan to evenly coat the bottom.

2. Add the ham along with the pepper and chopped onion and cook for a couple of minutes, frequently stirring.

3. Pour the eggs into the pan and while swirling back and for quickly over the heat, very swiftly, using a fork, stir to spread the eggs over the base of the pan as soon as they begin to thicken. Allow the pan to remain over the heat for 3 seconds to lightly brown the underside of the omelet. Take care not to overcook as the omelet with continue cooking once folded.

4. Carefully, while tilting the pan, run the fork under the edges of the omelet, jerking the pan to loosen the eggs from the bottom.

5. Fold the omelet closed, while bringing one side over the other and transfer to a plate.

Conclusion

I hope that you and those dining at your table will get to enjoy this collection of easy-to-follow Autumn recipes. These Autumn-based meals can help to warm you up on those cold chilly Autumn days! You can whip up any of these recipes without much fuss or muss in the preparing of these delightful meals. These are recipes that will help to bring a smile to a hungry face. I am sure you will enjoy that they are simple to prepare, so that will mean you will get to sit down and enjoy these classic Autumn recipes sooner than later!

www.ingramcontent.com/pod-product-compliance
Lightning Source LLC
Chambersburg PA
CBHW071845080526
44589CB00012B/1120